252
WE

LOVE
ONE
ANOTHER

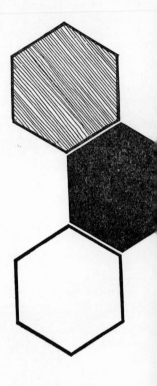

 **alba house**
A DIVISION OF ST. PAUL PUBLICATIONS
STATEN ISLAND, NEW YORK

LOVE
ONE
ANOTHER

SERMON OUTLINES FOR SUNDAYS AND HOLYDAYS
BY REVS. GERARD WEBER AND JAMES KILLGALLON
FOREWORD BY ALBERT CARDINAL MEYER

Nihil Obstat: Reverend Thomas F. Sullivan
Censor librorum

Imprimatur: Most Rev. Cletus F. O'Donnell, J.C.D.
Vicar General, Archdiocese of Chicago

February 11, 1965

Library of Congress Catalog Card No. 65 - 17978

Designed, printed and bound in the U.S.A. by the Pauline Fathers and Brothers as part of their communications apostolate.

Contents

CHARITY AND THE INDIVIDUAL — SEVEN SERMONS

Introduction

These sermon outlines, arranged for the Sundays and Holy Days of the year, are admirably planned according to aim, introduction, development and practical application. Ample background material is provided for the body of the sermon, and the whole is characterized by simplicity, timeliness and practicality.

Except for some on the major liturgical feasts and seasons, these sermon outlines are not necessarily linked to the Sundays of the year. Within the limits of the subject-matter divisions, the outlines may be re-arranged to suit the specific needs of the various dioceses. The order is not thereby affected, as each sermon is complete in itself. Those sermons, therefore, which are not appropriate to particular Sundays may be substituted by others without any difficulty.

This is particularly true of the "special sermons," whose date may vary from diocese to diocese and from year to year. For those dioceses where some of these special sermons may not be required at all, there are three additional outlines which may be taken instead. It is advisable that the special sermons be preached on the Sunday preceding that chosen for the topic to which the sermon refers, as is usually the case with letters from the diocesan authorities.

These sermon outlines were orginally prepared for use in the Archdiocese of Chicago. The first volume in the series was published by the Liturgical Press, Collegeville, Minn. and was titled "The God Who Loves Us." This volume treats of the way we respond to that love— by loving one another, and is aptly titled "Love One Another." The third volume in the series, "Liturgical Sermons," an elucidation of the Constitution on the Sacred Liturgy, has already appeared (Alba House). The fourth volume is in preparation—"Praise the Lord."

Foreword

The theme of these sermon outlines flows immediately from the great fact that God loves us and has made us His children.

We respond to God's love for us by loving God in return. But our love for God is inseparable from our love for each other. St. John says it with almost shocking directness, "If anyone says, 'I love God' and hates his brother, he is a liar" (I John 4:20). St. John, in the same Epistle, reminds us of what is so clearly and beautifully stated in his Gospel, that this is the great commandment which our Lord gave to His followers, that we love one another as He has first loved us, "And this is His commandment, that we should believe in the name of His Son Jesus Christ, and love one another, even as he gave us commandment" (I John 3:23).

Our Lord gave fraternal charity as the criterion by which we should be known as Christians, "By this will all men know that you are my disciples, if you have love for one another" (John 13:35). From the very beginning, therefore, the Church has taken to heart the words of the Master and has found ways to put into practice that fraternal charity which is the badge of a Christian. St. James early spelled out what the love of neighbor means in practice. He says, "Religion pure and undefiled before God the Father is this: to give aid to orphans and widows in their tribulation and to keep oneself unspotted from this world" (James 1:27). "And if a brother or sister be naked and in want of daily food and one of you say to them, 'Go in peace, be warmed and filled,' yet you do not give them what is necessary for the body, what does it profit? So faith too, unless it has works, is dead in itself" (James 2:15-17).

The earliest community of Christians, the Church in Jerusalem, showed a marvelous spirit of unity and love. No one among them was in want. The poor and widows were well cared for. Saints have risen up in every age who put Christian charity in the most practical terms by applying it to the problems which existed in their time. There were those who showed their love by giving themselves as ransom for captives. There were great apostles to neglected and homeless youth, like St. John Bosco. There were those who spent their lives caring for the sick and the poor, like St. Vincent de Paul. In every age the Church has preached and practiced the great commandment, the law of love.

In our day, too, the Church must and does continue to preach and practice love. Today, as she has always done in the past, the Church applies the principle of fraternal charity to the problems which confront us in our age. And tremendous problems they are, in this world of expanding populations, of emerging nations, of automation and technological revolution. There are problems of national proportion and there are great and pressing problems which are international. All these must be solved not only according to justice but also with real Christian fraternal charity.

No sermon outlines can even attempt to touch on all the problems of the day which require the attention and the love of all of us as Christians, but those in the present book do attempt to make a practical application of the law of love to some of the areas of modern life. What greater subject could we find on which to speak to our people than the love we have for one another as God's children? May the words we speak be themselves an expression of our own love.

✠ ALBERT CARDINAL MEYER
Archbishop of Chicago

FRATERNAL CHARITY — OUR RESPONSE TO GOD'S LOVE

aim: To explain the theme of these sermons — the fraternal love which, as Christians, we must have for one another. In our first volume (The Liturgical Press, Collegeville, Minn.) the theme was "The God who loves us." In this volume we shall dwell on the way we respond to God's love for us—by loving one another.

suggested introduction: Matth. 22:34-40. A doctor of the Law asks Jesus which is the greatest commandment of the Law. Our Lord answers by giving him not merely the first and greatest, the commandment which has to do with loving God, but also the second, the one which has to do with loving one's neighbor. Jesus thus shows that the two commandments are not to be separated.

development: 1. We must respond to God's love for us by loving one another. Our Lord said, "This is my commandment, that you love one another *as I have loved you.*" (John 15:12).

2. Our love for one another must be practical and effective, not merely a matter of words.

application: In these sermons we shall speak of the principles which underlie the practice of fraternal charity and apply them to daily life.

Background for Development:

introduction: St. Matthew's account of this incident (Matth. 22:34-40) gives the impression that the doctor of the Law was hostile to Jesus and insincere in asking which commandment was the greatest. St. Mark's account gives a different impression (Mk. 12:28-34). In Mark, the questioner is well-intentioned and sincerely asks a question which probably was the subject of debate in the schools.

In any event, the important point of the incident is that our Lord did not reply by merely stating that the commandment to love God was the most important. He added, "And the second is like it, 'Thou shalt love thy neighbor as thyself.'" The second is like it—i.e., love of neighbor is an overflow of the love of God, so much a part of love of God as to be inseparable from it.

1. Our Lord made it very clear that love of neighbor must go hand in hand with love of God. He summed up the whole Christian life by stating that it was a life of fraternal charity: "A new commandment I give you, that you love one another; that as I have loved you, you also love one another. By this will all men know that you are my disciples, if you have love for one another" (John 13:34-35).

St. John puts it very strongly: "If anyone says, I love God and hates his brother he is a liar. For how can he who does not love his brother, whom he sees, love God, whom he does not see?" (1 John 4:19-20).

It is easier to love what we can see, St. John tells us. On the other hand, it is often easier to love those we do not see. We are not annoyed by people who live far away from us and do not come into contact with us. But this is not really love; it does not have to prove itself. The test of our love of God is whether we really love the children of God. C. S. Lewis, in "The Screwtape Letters" has the devil give some shrewd advice to a younger devil who is on "tempting duty" on earth. The senior devil tells the tempter not to let his subject think about the beauty of God and of His mercy and goodness. He tells him to direct the man's attention to the people around him—the gossipy old lady, the dishonest butcher, the old fellow with warts on his neck, the people who never take a bath. Remind him that he has to love all these people too, the devil advises, so that he will see that it is no easy matter to love God.

2. On another occasion, when Jesus was speaking on the two great commandments, He described what it means to love one's neighbor. Cf. the parable of the Good Samaritan (Luke 10:25-37). Loving one's neighbor means more than feeling sorry for him. The priest and the Levite pitied the wounded man, no doubt, and wished, vaguely, that they could help him. But they weren't willing to go through any trouble to help him. They showed, therefore, that they did not really love him. The Samaritan showed that he did really love the wounded man. His love was real because it was effective and practical.

St. John says, "In this we have come to know His love that He laid down His life for us; and we likewise ought to lay down our life for the brethren. He who has the goods of this world and sees his brother in need and closes his heart to him, how does the love of God abide in him? My dear children, let us not love in word, neither with the tongue, but in deed and truth" (1 John 3:16-18).

Christ expresses, once again, the necessity of effective and practical love in His words about the last judgment. Here our Lord makes, what we have come to call the corporal and spiritual works of mercy, the sole criterion by which all men will be judged.

Charity which is effective and practical shows itself in action. It is not enough merely to pray for those who are underprivileged or who are suffering hardship. Fraternal charity requires that we try to do something about the plight of others. It requires that we help directly those who need help and are right at hand. It requires, too, that we be interested in the problems which affect human beings who are outside our immediate circle—problems such as unemployment and bad housing. It requires that we cooperate with others on many different levels in our everyday living.

application: The Bible and the teaching Church give us the general principles which we must follow in living according to the law of love. We ourselves must make the application of these principles to our daily life. During the liturgical year which begins today we shall speak of some of these principles, especially those which are taught by the popes in their social encyclicals. We shall speak of ways in which these principles can be applied in the concrete, when we meet our neighbors as individuals, when we meet them in our family, when we meet them as fellow members of our Church, of our community and of our nation.

SECOND SUNDAY OF ADVENT

THE NEW LAW OF LOVE

aim: To point out that we keep the laws of God and of His Church out of love for God and for our neighbor.

suggested introduction: The parable of the Pharisee and the publican (Luke 18:9-14) shows the spirit of the Pharisees, which Christ opposed so strongly.

development: 1. There is still the danger of falling into the error of thinking that the mere external keeping of laws will make one holy and pleasing to God.

2. We are no longer under the Mosaic Law, as were the Jews, but we have to keep the commandments as means of showing love for God and our neighbor and even to go beyond the commandments and live the law of love which Christ gave us.

3. Keeping a law is significant as a sign of love. Sin consists in failing to love.

application: We should ask ourselves not, "What am I bound to do or avoid under sin?" but "How can I show my love for my neighbor?" When we examine our conscience before Confession we should ask ourselves just one question, "How have I failed to show enough love for God and for my neighbor?" We will then see our sins for what they are, not merely the breaking of a law but a failure to love.

Background for Development:

introduction: Very prominent among the groups who resisted Christ, opposed His teachings and sought to destroy Him were many members of the powerful sect, the Pharisees. Reason enough for their opposition could be found in the parable of the Pharisee and the publican (Luke 18:9-14). Luke prefaces this parable which shows the pride and self-deceit of some Pharisees with the words, "But he spoke this parable also to some who trusted in themselves and despised others. . . ." Christ was constantly unmasking the hypocrisy of the Pharisees and upbraiding them for their legalism. They, in turn, hated Him, tried to trip Him up and were prominent in the movement to silence Him and put Him to death.

The word Pharisee has become so closely associated with hypocrisy, legalism and sterile formalism that many people forget that the sect began as a good and praiseworthy thing. Originally, the Pharisees strove to bring the people back to a careful observance of the Mosaic Law. The Law was to be observed in every detail, but it was to be observed with love, as a sign of a man's love of God and loyalty to Him. Later, the Pharisees fell into the error of thinking that merely keeping the Law in their external actions would make them holy and pleasing to God. They forget that the Law was to be kept as a sign of love. They came to despise their fellow men. They loaded burdens upon the people by the exaggerated strictness with which they interpreted the Law. They had contempt for the poor and the unlearned. They hated Christ because He loved the humble, common people and championed their cause.

1. The Pharisees as a sect have disappeared, but the error into which they fell still exists and presents a danger—the error of thinking that the mere observance of a law can in itself make one holy and pleasing to God. It is only love that can make one pleasing to God. The keeping of a law is significant as a sign of love of God, and of one's neighbor. The Christian, too, must observe the laws of God and of the Church, but he must be careful not to fall into the error of the Pharisees. He must not think that the mere keeping of laws is all that is expected of him. He must keep the spirit of the law and not merely its letter.

2. With the coming of Christ, the Old Law gave way to the New Law. The Mosaic Law is unnecessary for the Christian, just as a tutor

becomes unnecessary when the child has grown up. Before Christ, the children of God were children, "in bondage," as St. Paul says, under the Law. The Christian, with the full revelation of Jesus Christ and the new life which Christ has given him in Baptism, has been set free by Christ.

St. Paul says that Christians are "not under the law." This was the great decision which the Apostles made in council at Jerusalem. Obviously, this does not mean that the Christian does not have to keep the ten commandments. What it does mean is that the Christian life is not circumscribed by the ten commandments, that the norm for the Christian is something beyond the ten commandments. The Christian is bound to God not by a law, as were the Jews, but by a person, Jesus Christ. The Christian, while he observes all the precepts of the basic moral law, looks for guidance and inspiration not to that law but to the Holy Spirit, dwelling within him. The law which the Christian has to observe is just one commandment—the commandment of love. Jesus expressed it very clearly at the Last Supper. "A new commandment I give you, that you love one another; that as I have loved you, you also love one another. By this will all men know that you are my disciples, if you have love for one another" (John 13:34-35).

The Christian must obey the commandments and the laws of the Church, but he obeys them out of love, realizing that his obedience is not just compliance with a law but a manifestation of his love for God and for his neighbor. He sees the commandments as laws which define the outer limits of the practice of love of God and of one's neighbor. His model is Jesus Christ. His norm of behavior is the love of Christ. He seeks to love all men as Christ loves all men.

3. Some people are so pre-occupied with the letter of the laws which bind them that they forget the meaning of the laws. They come to think that it is sinful to fail to keep a law or to break it unknowingly. They think that they are guilty of sin if they missed Mass, even though they were sick in bed. They think that they must confess eating meat on Friday even though they did not know it was Friday when they ate the meat. These people forget that sin consists not in failing to observe a law but in failing to love. The sin is not in eating meat on Friday. I might have done so unknowingly. The sin is in not loving God by preferring meat to His will deliberately. The sin is not in injuring my neighbor. I might have injured him by accident. The sin is in not loving my neighbor and therefore injuring him deliberately. All sin is simply lack of love—of God or of one's neighbor.

application: Nothing is more alien to the spirit of religion which Jesus preached and lived than legalism, preoccupation with the letter of the law, making our religion a matter of laws to be kept and obligations to be met rather than a new life as children of God and brothers in Christ. Yet, there is a tendency to legalism in all of us. We must strive to see sin for what it is—a failure to love. We must strive to see laws as means of showing love. We should not have as our norm of behavior, "Is it a sin?" but rather, "How can I show love for God and my neighbor?" We should not ask, "What am I bound to do?" but rather, "What would Christ do?" In examining our conscience we should seek to discover how our behavior has been, not in relation to laws but in relation to love.

FEAST OF THE IMMACULATE CONCEPTION

OUR LADY AND FRATERNAL CHARITY

aim: To show that our Blessed Lady is a model of fraternal charity. If we truly love Mary we will love our neighbor and seek to help others as she does.

suggested introduction: The story of the marriage feast of Cana shows the kindness and charity of our Blessed Mother.

development: 1. During her life on earth, our Lady was always alert to the needs of others, and did all she could to help them.

2. From heaven our Lady continues to show her love for all God's children whom she loves as her own children.

application: As true children of our Blessed Mother we must show our love for all men by being interested in them and helping them.

Background for Development:

introduction: At the marriage feast of Cana it was Mary who first noticed that the wine was running out. Her first thought was for the young bridal couple. They would be embarrassed and ashamed before all their friends. Mary's reaction was immediate. She came to the rescue of the young couple by bringing the matter to the attention of Jesus. This charming story brings out the kindness and charity of our Blessed Mother and shows the concern she has for others.

1. The Immaculate Conception emphasizes the tremendous sanctity of Mary, the holiest of all human persons. The *fact* of Mary's holiness is something which we realize very well. What we might not realize well enough is the *nature* of our Lady's sanctity. We know that Mary was completely sinless. We must not conclude that she was holy only in the sense that she never offended God in the slightest way. Mary's holiness is an intensely positive thing. It is a reflection of the holiness of Christ. Christ's holiness was expressed most perfectly in His own words, "Not my will but thine be done"— Mary's in her words, "Behold the handmaid of the Lord; be it done to me according to thy word." But Christ's love of His Father expressed itself also in His tremendous love for all men. His life is summed up in the words, "He went about doing good." Mary's holiness, by the same token, was not merely a matter of quiet absorption in prayer, apart from the lives of other people. Like Christ, she was deeply involved with others. Like Him, she expressed her love for God by her great love for all God's children. Her response to God's love was to love her neighbor.

According to tradition, our Lady remained with the apostles during the early years of the Church in Jerusalem, as a source of inspiration and guidance. During those years she was, beyond doubt, a great model of fraternal charity to the whole Christian community.

2. We call our Lady "Help of Christians" and "Comforter of the Afflicted." These titles express the role which Mary plays even as she reigns with Christ in glory. She is still a model of charity, making constant intercession for all her children. In the "Memorare" we say, "Never was it known that anyone who fled to your assistance, implored your help or sought your interecession was left unaided." The Church teaches that Mary intercedes for us even when we do not directly ask for her intercession. She is sensitive to even the small needs of people, just as she was at Cana.

The many apparitions of Mary are another proof of her great charity. Again and again she has come with a message of love from her divine Son. She has come to call upon Christians for prayer, asking for repentance from sin and a renewal of Christian life; always she repeats the message of Christ, "Love God and love one another."

application: Mary expects her children to imitate her in her love for others. It is not enough to say we love our Lady and to pray to her. We must put fraternal charity into practice.

In his encyclical, written on the occasion of the first centenary of the appearance of Mary at Lourdes, Pius XII says: "The faithful must rally round their priests and collaborate in this effort for a renewal of Christian life. Let them ask themselves whether they could not do something more for the cause of God in that place, in those circles, where His providence has placed them. . . . Our thoughts turn at the same time to Christian families, to adjure them to remain faithful to their irreplaceable mission in society. Let them in this jubilee year consecrate themselves to the Immaculate Heart of Mary. This act of piety will be a precious help to them in their duty of chastity and conjugal fidelity and will preserve the atmosphere of purity in the home where children are growing up. More, it will make the family, revitalized by devotion to Mary, a living cell in the social body, working from within for its regeneration. Beyond the family circle, professional and civic contacts also afford to Christians who are anxious to work for the renewal of society a vast field of action. Gathering at the feet of Mary and ready to learn from her, they will first of all make a searching examination of conscience and root out from their hearts false judgments and selfishness. We have reason to fear that we are acting a lie if our love of God does not translate itself into an effective love of our brothers. Christians of all classes and nations must unite themselves in truth and charity, laying aside mutual misunderstandings and suspicions."

THIRD SUNDAY OF ADVENT

ST. PAUL DESCRIBES CHARITY

aim: To explain St. Paul's words on the necessity of charity and its qualities. (1 Cor. Chapter 13)

suggested introduction: The situation in Corinth which prompted St. Paul to write his famous words on the gift of charity.

development: In his letter St. Paul, first of all, points out the utter necessity of charity.

2. St. Paul describes the qualities of true charity.

application: We should measure our love of neighbor against the yard-stick which St. Paul gives.

Background for Development:

introduction: There was dissent among the Christians at Corinth in the middle of the first century A.D. Some of them found themselves in possession of those strange charismatic gifts which manifested themselves in the very early days of Christianity. Some who had no such gifts at all were jealous of those who had them.

Some, who had, say, the gift of tongues, were envious of others who had the power of interpreting or of prophecy. In the midst of all the wrangling and disputing which was going on, these early Christians were forgetting the most important gift of all. In their anxiety to possess the relatively unimportant and transitory charismatic gifts, they undervalued the great and all-important gift, the gift of charity, which every Christian must possess and which is his badge as a Christian.

The dispute was brought to the attention of St. Paul, who was at Ephesus at the time. Paul wrote to the Corinthians, reminding them of the primacy of charity. In this letter is Paul's magnificent passage in praise of charity. The Apostle not only explains the utter necessity of charity, he describes in detail what love of neighbor is and how it shows itself (Cf. I Cor. Chapter 13).

1. St. Paul begins by pointing out that the charismatic gifts, which seem so spectacular, are utterly worthless unless one has the all important gift, the gift of charity. The gift of tongues, without charity, is just empty words, just meaningless sounds. The gift of prophecy, the gift of knowledge which could even penetrate to the heart of the mysteries of the faith, are worthless without charity. Even faith avails nothing without charity. Jesus said that if a man's faith were great enough he could move a mountain. Paul points out that a man with faith even so great as all that, is simply nothing if he does not also have charity. Jesus said that in order to be perfect we should be poor in spirit. "Go, sell what thou hast, and give to the poor, and thou shalt have treasure in heaven," He said to the rich young man who asked how he could gain eternal life. But this idea supposes that the one who gives all his possessions to the poor does so out of love. If he does not have charity, his seeming generosity will gain him no reward from God. "If I distribute all my goods to feed the poor . . . yet do not have charity," says St. Paul, "it profits me nothing." Jesus said that anyone who would lay down his life for Him would find it. To give one's life in martyrdom has always been regarded as an act which merits heaven immediately. But even giving up one's life is not martyrdom unless it is done out of love. St. Paul says, "If I deliver my body to be burned, yet do not have charity, it profits me nothing."

2. Having shown the necessity of charity, St. Paul goes on to describe its qualities. It is easy enough to say that you love your neighbor. But that is not enough. Love of neighbor must show itself in practice.

"Charity is patient," says St. Paul. How often people, under the guise of charity, are impatient with others for not measuring up to what they expect of them. How often people hurt others by losing patience and snapping at them. True love of neighbor shows itself by patience, even, with another's faults and shortcomings.

"Charity is kind," How often people hurt others by slighting them, by ignoring them, by speaking or acting in an unkind manner. How often people hurt others, telling themselves that they are really doing it for the other person's good, when actually they are merely being unkind.

"Charity does not envy." One who really loves his neighbor is genuinely glad to see good fortune come to him. Envy is a sign of selfishness and lack of love for another.

"Charity is not pretentious, is not puffed, is not ambitious." One who truly loves his neighbor does not try to impress him with his importance. To do so is really to put the other fellow down a peg and make him feel inferior. It is a sign of self-love, as is ambition, the desire to get ahead of others, to dominate others.

"Charity is not self-seeking." Love seeks the good of the other person, even prefers the good of the other to one's own. The first requirement of love is that it is unselfish. The uncharitable person shows his selfishness by always taking the best thing for himself, whether it is a seat on the bus, the choicest piece of meat on the platter or a chance to express his opinion in a conversation.

"Charity is not provoked; thinks no evil, does not rejoice over wickedness, but rejoices with the truth." Love for our neighbor requires that we keep our temper, that we try to realize that the other person is upset and refrain from fighting fire with fire. Love requires, too, that we judge others kindly, not imputing motives, not listening to rumors about the behavior of others or entering into un unkind discussion of their faults. One who really loves his neighbor does not feel a "righteous" satisfaction when the other person has to suffer because of his sins. He does not say, "It serves him right." Instead, he feels pity, and does what he can to ease the suffering.

"Charity bears with all things, believes all things, hopes all things, endures all things." One who loves his neighbor puts up with the faults of his neighbor. He takes unkindness and thoughtlessness, trying to realize that he, too, has his faults, seeking to find reasons to account for the other person's behavior and to find excuses for him, as people always do for themselves. He believes the best of his neighbor and encourages him to do his best and to become better.

application: It is easy to deceive ourselves into thinking that we are practicing love for our neighbor when we are really not. We should be lenient in our judgments of other people, but strict and honest in examining our own motives. We should measure our love of neighbor against the yard-stick which the Holy Spirit gives us through St. Paul.

WE MUST LOVE ONE ANOTHER BECAUSE WE DEPEND ON ONE ANOTHER

aim: To give as one of the motives of our love for others the fact that men were created by God to depend on one another.

suggested introduction: The Gospels show us that Jesus came as a man into a complex human world. Our Lord depended on others, as all men do.

development: 1. All human beings have a great dependence on one another.

2. God made men dependent on one another so that they would love one another.

application: The Christian must love all men because they are God's children, because he sees Christ in them. Nonetheless, it is important to remember that there is a natural basis for love of neighbor—the great inter-dependence which exists among human beings.

Background for Development:

introduction: St. Matthew's Gospel begins with a long genealogy, which, sketchy as it is, takes up sixteen verses and impresses on us the fact that Christ was born of a people whose roots stretched back into antiquity. St. Luke, in just two verses, gives us a glimpse of the complicated political structure in which Jesus lived.

"Now in the fifteenth year of the reign of Tiberius Caesar, when Pontius Pilate was procurator of Judea, and Herod tetrarch of Galilee, and Philip his brother tetrarch of the district of Iturea and Trachonitis and Lysanias tetrarch of Abilina, during the high priesthood of Annas and Caiphas, the word of God came to John, the son of Zachary in the desert" (Luke 3:1-3).

When St. John the Baptist pointed to a young carpenter who walked along the banks of the Jordan and said, "Behold the Lamb of God," his listeners knew what he meant. If this man was the long awaited Promised One, He did not appear out of nowhere, without any preparation. He did not suddenly materialize among the people, a man without a family, without a nation, without relatives or ancestors. He was born into the family of Mary of Nazareth and Joseph, the carpenter. He was born in Bethlehem, the ancestral home of all the descendants of David. He was born a Jew and a subject of the Roman

Empire. He grew up amid the community life of a small Galilean town. He spoke Aramaic, the language of His people and His town. He had come only after centuries and centuries of preparation during which God had used patriarchs, kings and prophets to set the stage for His coming.

Christ depended completely on Mary and Joseph during His infancy. He had all the normal dependencies of a man, living in human society. He depended on John the Baptist to act as His precursor. He depended on the disciples He chose and sent to preach in the towns and villages throughout the country. He depended on the Apostles to spread the Church throughout the world. He depended on His friends for companionship and consolation, and was disappointed when they failed him, as the Apostles did during His agony in the garden. He depended on the people who showed Him hospitality, like Martha and Mary, and on the dedicated women who followed Him about and ministered to Him. In all these things, Christ emphasized the fact that men need one another and therefore have obligations to one another.

1. It has been said that if a man paused for a moment before eating a piece of bread and thought of the number of people who had been involved in producing that bread and bringing it to his table, he would eat it with a certain amount of awe and reverence. We know in a general way, of course, that as human beings we are inter-dependent, but we often fail to realize how complete this dependence is. It comes home to us when a crippling strike occurs, or when we are reminded by a T. V. program such as "What's My Line" of an occupation to which we have never averted but which serves the needs of millions of human beings.

A human infant is the most helpless being in the world. At the outset, man is totally dependent on others, not only on his parents but also on their doctor, their grocer, their milkman and the dozens of people whose services make civilized life possible. All men need the help of many others in order to grow and develop physically, intellectually and spiritually. The various institutions of society exist in order to assist in man's development—the family, the city, the state, the federal government, the school system, the economic and social order. Even the institutions which provide recreation are necessary for a man's development and health. In his religious life, too, man needs his fellow man. No one can baptize himself. A man needs another man in order to receive the divine life of grace. Man needs his fellow man in order to worship God in the Mass. He needs his fellow man in order to learn of God and to live the Christian life. Here, as in everything else, there is the greatest inter-dependence.

2. God has made men dependent on one another for a reason. He wants men to love one another. The human race is a family. The human

race is one. God never forgets this great fact, even if men themselves do. God made man in such a way that he must by his very nature live with and in cooperation with his fellow man, fulfilling his duties and acknowledging the rights of others. Pius XI in his encyclical on the reconstruction of the social order said that it is only a man living in an orderly society—that is, in cooperation with others—who can attain life here on earth in preparation for a happy eternity. St. Thomas Aquinas says that the inclination to live peaceably in society is just as much a part of human nature as the inclination for self-preservation, for marriage and parenthood and the inclination of the mind to seek truth.

Because man needs his fellow man, he must love him. Human beings must live together in peace and harmony for the good of everyone. Since the human race is a family, men must live as members of a family.

application: Even if it were not for the great supernatural reasons which underlie fraternal charity, men would still be obliged to love one another because of the natural motive—the fact that God has made the human race as a family. Many people out of sheer humanitarianism have given great examples of love for their fellow man. The Christian has much more compelling reasons for loving his neighbor, He sees Christ Himself in his neighbor. He loves him not merely as a fellow man but as his brother in Christ and as one of God's children. Nevertheless, even as Christians, we should not forget that there is a basis for love of neighbor in human nature itself.

CHRISTMAS DAY

THE DIGNITY WHICH IS MAN'S BECAUSE GOD BECAME MAN

aim: To bring about an appreciation of the dignity of man and show how God has enhanced that dignity by taking human nature to Himself.

suggested introduction: A nineteenth century poet cried out to God, "What do you know of our woes, you in your well lighted sky?" The Incarnation, above all, shows how false a statement this is.

development: 1. Even by nature, man has great dignity as the lord of creation, made in the image of God.

2. By becoming man, God raised man far above the angels. Men are now blood brothers of Christ, called to be sons of God through Christ.

3. Christmas is the great feast which recalls to us the love we should have for one another and the peace of Christ which should prevail among men.

application: On Christmas we should pray that we may be peacemakers, and resolve to treat all human beings according to their great dignity.

Background for Development:

introduction: A nineteenth century poet, distressed by the miserable condition of the coal miners who toiled in the dark and dirty mines from dawn to dusk, wrote a poem addressed to God, in which he complained, "What do you know of our woes, you in your well-lighted sky?" Any child who has studied his catechism could have told this poet how wrong he was. God is everywhere. He is down in the mines, dwelling amidst and within the miners who work in their dark depths. But the complete refutation of this charge that God is aloof from His world and does not involve Himself in the affairs of men is to be found in the Christmas crib. Each year we are confronted again with the marvelous fact of God's love for us as we come in spirit to the stable at Bethlehem at Christmas and contemplate the staggering truth that the most high God took to Himself a human body and soul and became a man. This fact gives to the human race a new worth and dignity which is incalulable.

1. Psalm 8 speaks of the natural worth and dignity of a human being. Speaking of man, the psalmist sings, "You have made him a little less than the angels, and crowned him with glory and honor.

You have given him rule over the works of your hands, putting all things under his feet:

All sheep and oxen, yes, and the beasts of the field,

The birds of the air, the fishes of the sea, and whatever swims the paths of the sea."

This is an echo of the words of God Himself in the first chapter of the book of Genesis: "Let us make mankind in our image and likeness; and let them have dominion over the fish of the sea, the birds of the air, the cattle, over all the wild animals and every creature that crawls on the earth" (Gen. 1:26)

Man, even by nature, is a truly wonderful being. He is the lord of creation. He alone, of all God's creatures, lives in the midst of God's creation, seeing the wonders that God has made, knowing them for what they are, the work of God's hands, and using them as the steward of God's possessions. Only he, of all the beings on the earth, can truly know and love. Only he can raise his heart and mind to God in prayer. Only he can produce civilization, art, science—all the things which bring God's creation to ever greater stages of perfection. Truly, man is a sharer in the creativity of Almighty God.

The Judaeo-Christian concept of man has always been an exalted one. Man is not, like the beasts, merely a material thing which will die and pass out of existence. Man is a truly wonderful and unique creature, a composite of matter and spirit. Western civilization has always regarded every human life as a very precious thing. Even today there is a world of difference between the attitude of the free world and the materialistic communistic word as to the worth of each human being and his dignity as a person.

Even if the Incarnation had never taken place, therefore, man's dignity and worth would be very great. Men would still have to respect one another and live as brothers, as befits human dignity.

2. But the Incarnation has taken place. God Himself has chosen to become a member of the human race. Man is no longer "a little less than the angels;" he has been raised far above the angels by the fact that his nature has been united to God in the God-man, Jesus Christ. St. Thomas put it forth as a possibility that the rebellion of Satan and his angels was occasioned by a revelation from God that one day His Son would unite the divine nature, not to the angelic, but to the human. This could well have been too much for those proud spirits. They realized the heights to which God has raised man by the Incarnation of the Divine Word. Man is no longer merely a wonderful creature, made in the image of God; he is now a blood brother of the Son of God. Through Christ he is an adopted son of God, destined to share God's life forever. He has been purchased by the blood of Christ. No limit can be placed on his value. St. Paul says, "Do you know that your members are the temple of the Holy Spirit, who is in you, whom you have from God, and that you are not your own? For you have been bought at a great price. Glorify God and bear him in your body" (1 Cor. 6:19-20).

Christmas is recognized by all as the great feast of love. It is a time when men stop for a short time and consider the great fact that all men are brothers, that all men belong to the family of God. God has always seen the whole human race as one. Adam was not merely a man; he was a man. He was the head of the race. In him the entire human race offended God and separated themselves from God. Christ is the New Adam, the new head of the race. He is the Son of Man.

In Him the entire human race is re-united to God. Through Christ all men are brothers in the deepest sense, brothers of His and of each other and children of God, His Father. As brothers, realizing the great dignity that each man has because of Christ, all men are to love each other as Christ has loved each of them.

Christmas is recognized by all, too, as the great feast of peace. On this feast we celebrate the coming among us of the Prince of Peace. The angels in the sky over Bethlehem proclaimed peace on earth. The feast of Christmas impels people to put aside quarrels and differences and to enjoy, for a short while, the harmony and peace which should exist among brothers in Christ. The pity is that it is only for a day, only at Christmas, that so many men catch a glimpse of their brotherhood with all other men.

application: We should pray for peace in the world at all times, but especially at Christmas, the feast of peace. We should also work for peace, peace among the people we live with and work with. It is difficult to fight with a person who refuses to fight back, who responds with cheerfulness and kindness to rudeness and hostility. Responding this way is part of being a peacemaker. We should do everything we can to bring about peace and harmony among men by our Christian attitude in regard to racial prejudice and discrimination.

SUNDAY AFTER CHRISTMAS

WHAT WE DO TO OTHERS
WE DO TO CHRIST

aim: To show the supernatural basis for love of neighbor, the identification of Christ with the members of His Mystical Body.

suggested introduction: Our Lord's description of the last judgment and His words,—"As long as you did it for one of these, the least of my brethren, you did it for me" (Cf. Matt. 25: 31-40).

development: 1. Our faith teaches us that Jesus Christ has taken to Himself a new Body, the Church. He is inseparable from that Body.

2. The Mystical Body provides us with the real basis for fraternal

charity. It explains why love of neighbor is inseparable from love of God—love of Christ.

> **application:** The test of our love of Christ is the way we treat our neighbor.

Background for Development:

> **introduction:** Every time we say the Apostles' Creed we pronounce a phrase that expresses a great event to which we modern Catholics do not often advert—"He shall come again to judge the living and the dead"—the final, glorious coming of Christ at the end of the world. Our Lord Himself describes this event: "But when the Son of Man shall come in his majesty, and all the angels with him, then he will sit on the throne of his glory; and before Him will be gathered all the nations, and he will separate them one from another, as the shepherd separates the sheep from the goats; and he will set the sheep on his right hand, but the goats on his left. Then the King will say to those on his right hand, "Come, blessed of my Father, take possession of the kingdom prepared for you from the foundation of the world; for I was hungry and you gave me to eat; I was thirsty and you gave me to drink; I was a stranger and you took me in; naked and you covered me; sick and you visited me; I was in prison and you came to me. Then the just will answer him, saying, 'Lord, when did we see thee hungry and feed thee; or thirsty and gave thee drink? And when did we see thee a stranger and take thee in; or naked and clothe thee? Or when did we see thee sick or in prison, and come to thee?' And answering the king will say to them, 'Amen I say to you, as long as you did it for one of these, the least of my brethren, you did it for me' " (Matth. 25:31:40).

1. The words of our Lord, "As long as you did it for one of these, the least of my brethren, you did it for me," express a truth far more profound than would be apparent to the uninitiated, to those who do not know the doctrine of the Mystical Body of Christ. For them, these words would mean only that Jesus will *count* as having been done personally to Him whatever we do to anyone of His followers. This, in itself, would be strong enough, but we know that the words have a much stronger meaning. They mean that whatever we do to another we actually do to Christ because we do it to one who is joined to Him in the unity of His Mystical Body. We see this same reality underlying the words which Jesus spoke from heaven to St. Paul at the moment of his miraculous conversion on the road to Damascus, "Saul, Saul, why dost thou persecute *me?*" It is significant that St. Paul did not make any objection to this question. He did ask one question, a natural the logical one—"Who art thou, Lord?" But when Jesus replied, "I

am Jesus, whom thou art persecuting," Paul did not retort that he was persecuting not Jesus personally but the members of His Church. Perhaps Paul did not make this objection because in that flash, with the grace of conversion, there might have been given to him the first revelation of the great doctrine which he preached, ever more clearly and forcefully, throughout the rest of his life, the oneness of Christ and His members in the Mystical Body of Christ.

The doctrine of the Mystical Body teaches us that we must distinguish between two meanings of the words "Christ" or "Jesus." Jesus, or Christ, as a lone individual, the God-man who preached in the streets of Jerusalem—the physical Christ or the historical Christ—is our Lord as He was during His life on earth nearly 2,000 years ago. Jesus, or Christ, in His fullness, the glorified Christ who rose from the dead and sits at the right hand of the Father, is inseparable from the millions whom He has taken to Himself by baptizing them into His new body, the Mystical Body. Christ, as He is today, is the Head of this Body, which He took to Himself as He died on the cross. He cannot be separated from that Body. We cannot go to Him except through that Body. We cannot love Him unless we love the whole Body whose Head He is. We cannot love Him unless we love every single member of that Body.

2. The great commandment of Christ is that we must love one another; we must return the love He has for us, and we must love one another. The fact of the Mystical Body of Christ explains the real reason why love of neighbor is inseparable from love of Christ, love of God. Our neighbor *is* Christ, since he is a member of Christ's Body. And, people should perhaps be reminded, in practice everyone, whether he belongs to the visible Church or not, is to be treated as a member of the Mystical Body. Therefore, whenever we look into the eyes of another man, we are looking into the eyes of Christ. Whenever we talk to or listen to another human being, we are talking to or listening to Christ. We see Christ all around us every day. We may not think of Him simply as the glorified Savior, reigning peacefully in heaven, or even as our Savior living among us in the Eucharist. Christ walks the streets; He shops in the supermarkets; He drives the car in the next lane; He lives on Lake Shore Drive and in the overcrowded ghettos in which segregation confines Him. Christ feels hunger and cold today. He feels injustices and affronts to human dignity. He feels the warmth and kindness of brotherly love. He feels whatever the members of His Mystical Body feel, because He lives, acts and reacts in each of those members.

application: Charity would be easy if it were merely a matter of loving God, of loving the God-man, Jesus Christ. God is perfect; Christ is the perfect man. There are no faults there,

no ugliness, no unpleasantness, no ingratitude. The Mystical Body
shows us the harsh reality. If we want to love the Christ who preached
the Sermon on the Mount we must love Him as we meet Him in every
human contact today. And the Christ we meet in our daily life is not
perfect. He is often not at all easy to love. Nevertheless, we have no
choice; in order to love Christ we must love every member of Christ,
every potential member, every human being. And the test of our love
is how we treat Christ in our neighbor, what we do or fail to do to him.

THE USE OF TIME

aim: To recall the fact that time is a precious gift
God gives us to use in our development for heaven, and to point
out how this gift might be better used.

suggested introduction: The dawn of the New
Year reminds us of how swiftly time passes. It should make us pause
and consider the value of time.

development: 1. Time is the period God gives
us in which to prepare for our eternal destiny.

2. Our Lord and the saints show us how time should be used.

3. One of the best uses we can make of time is to give it to others.
Such a gift is a real act of charity.

application: Each should reflect on the way
he uses time every day.

Background for Development:

introduction: Each New Year's Day the news-
papers depict the new year as a robust but very young child. The old
year, on the other hand, is a doddering old figure with a long white
beard. It is always amusing, but also somewhat frightening, to realize
that this year's old man was last year's baby and that the healthy, vital,
hopeful child who is this new year will, in just 365 days, be another
bent old figure, tottering towards the grave.

Each New Year's Day is a milestone in our life. It brings home to us
the swiftness of the passage of time. It should make us pause for a

moment and think of the meaning of time itself and its relationship to eternity.

1. We are well aware of the distinction between time and eternity. Those who are living in time are "in via." Those in eternity are "in termino." There is no possibility of meriting, no chance for penance, no opportunity of changing anything once we have passed into eternity. All this can take place only in time. Time, whatever its philosophical definition, is the period God gives us in which to prepare for eternity. God has destined us for a life in eternity for which we are totally unfitted by nature; He has destined us to enter into the very life of the Holy Trinity, to share the life of God Himself. He gives us the divine life of sanctifying grace in this life in order that we may increase in it day by day, year by year and so develop as to be ready to enter heaven when we die. Every moment of our life in time, every moment of the period when we are "in via," is meant to be used to further our development for eternity. God has given us the gift of time in order that we might develop and bring to full maturity all the powers He has given us. The more talent God has given us, the more He expects in the way of development. The more grace we have received, the more God will expect in the way of holiness. This fact is brought out clearly by our Lord in the parable of the talents (Cf. Matth. 25:14-30).

2. Our mind tells us, therefore, that time is a very precious thing, something to be used profitably and carefully, never to be wasted. Yet we often go to a lot of trouble finding ways of wasting time. We say, "What shall I do to kill time for the next couple of hours?" Without becoming a fanatic or a crank, without becoming scrupulous about it, a Christian ought to have a higher regard for time. The saints were not fanatics, nor were they scrupulous or unreasonable. They simply loved God so much that they found the time at their disposal all too short to manifest that love. They made time for prayer no matter how busy they were. And they were very busy, because, loving their neighbor as they did, they found the time they had all too short to serve Christ in him. St. Alphonsus took a vow never to waste a minute of time. This might be regarded as rather an extreme; surely it is something which is out of order for the ordinary person. But it is not necessary to take a vow. All that is necessary to grow in the love of God and neighbor. Anyone who does will find that he hasn't near enough time to do all that needs to be done.

Our Lord gives us the perfect example of the use of time. He came to do the will of His Father. He regarded the time He had at His disposal as very precious. It was God's time, and He used it in the service of God. "I must do the works of Him who sent Me while it is day," Christ told His apostles. "Night is coming when no man can work" (John 9:4). Jesus found time to rest and to recreate. He attended the marriage feast of Cana. He went to dinner in the home of people who invited Him. He was often in the home of Martha and Mary and Lazarus, visiting with them. But we know that our Lord never wasted time. Wherever He was and whatever He was doing, it was the will of God He was doing. This, precisely, is the proper use of time. If it is God's will that here and now I should be selling insurance or ironing clothes I would be misusing time by running off to church to make the stations. If it is time for recreation I am doing God's will by taking recreation and therefore using time properly. It is only when recreation or rest becomes excessive and interferes with work, with prayer, or with the development I must make of my faculties that it constitutes a waste of time.

3. One of the best uses of time is to give it to others. How often people refuse to do an act of kindness on the plea that they do not have the time? Our Lord always found the time to help others. It is easier to give money than it is to give time. Giving time involves a giving of oneself much more than does the giving of money. Taking a little time just to listen to others, to give attention to them, can be an act of real charity.

application: There is one resolution which everyone ought to make, one which it would be possible to keep—the resolution to make better use of our time. A general resolution will not be effective. If it is to be practical and effective it must be particularized. First of all, we should reflect on how we use our time. Everyone will find that there is some time during the day which is wasted. It may be the time we spend riding the bus or the train. It may be the time we spend reading every bit of newsprint in the papers. It may be the time we spend watching the late show on television, mesmerized by an old movie we would not walk across the street to see in a theatre. Whatever it is, if we resolved to spend even ten or fifteen minutes of that time reading something of value, something spiritual or something which is at least worth while, we would be doing something to improve the use we make of our time.

FEAST OF THE HOLY NAME OF JESUS

THE HOLY NAME

aim: To show that real love for the Holy Name entails not only refraining from using it with irreverence but also praying in the name of Jesus and bringing Christ into the world in which one lives.

suggested introduction: St. Peter cured a lame beggar by using the name of Jesus. He told the people that it was in the power of that name that this miracle was wrought.

development: 1. There is much more involved in respect for the name of Jesus than merely avoiding using it in vain. We should also pray in the name of Jesus, as the Church does.

2. Love for the name of Jesus also requires that we take part in the Church's work of bringing Christ and His teachings into every part of life.

application: In order to take part in the Church's work of bringing Christ to the world we must learn the teachings of Christ in their modern application and we must acquire the mind and heart of Christ by reading the Scriptures with faith and love.

Background for Development:

introduction: The words of St. Peter, which we find in the First Scripture Reading of today's Mass, were spoken by Peter in explanation of a miracle which he had worked the day before and which had been the occasion of his and John's arrest. Peter and John had been about to enter the temple when a lame beggar, who was being carried to his usual spot at the gate of the temple, called out to them, asking for alms. Peter said, "Silver and gold I have none; but what I have, that I give thee. In the name of Jesus Christ of Nazareth, arise and walk." The man was instantly cured and went with Peter and John into the temple, "walking and leaping and praising God." Peter explained to the people, who were full of wonder at this miracle, that it was by the power of the name of Jesus that the man had been healed: "It is his name, by means of faith in his name, that has made strong this man whom you behold and recognize..." (Cf. Acts 3:1-16).

1. The Feast of the Holy Name of Jesus has a special appeal for Catholic men. In Catholic parishes the Holy Name Society is the organization for the men of the parish. One of the objectives of this organization is to foster respect for the name of Jesus. There is much more involved in respect for the name of Jesus than merely not using it in vain. To use the Holy Name in vain would be a slight irreverence, a venial, not a mortal sin. Nevertheless, it is something which is particularly offensive to those who are truly followers of Christ. We should, however, see the important positive aspects of respect for the

name of Jesus. Our Lord told the Apostles that they were to pray to the Father in His name. We are not simply to refrain from using the name of Jesus in vain, therefore; we are to use it with great faith and reverence when we pray. The usual way in which the Church prays in her liturgy is to the Father, through His Son Jesus Christ Our Lord, in union with the Holy Spirit. Here the Church is giving all her children an example which they might well follow in their private prayers.

But respect for the name of Jesus entails more than using it in our prayers. The love and loyalty that we have for Our Lord should make us anxious to make His name known by all men, and make us want to bring the knowledge and love of Jesus Christ to others.

2. It was God Himself who gave the name of Jesus to His Son when He became man. The Archangel Gabriel said to Mary at the Annunciation, "Thou shalt call his name Jesus" (Luke 1:31).

The giving of a name has always been a matter of importance in the history of salvation. God changed Abram's name to Abraham and his wife Saris' to Sara. He changed Jacob's name to Israel. Jesus changed Simon's name to Peter when He promised to give him the primacy in His Church. God gave names which signified the role which this person was to play in His plan of salvation. Jesus, the name which God gave to His Son at His conception, means "savior," as was explained to St. Joseph in a dream. (Cf. Matth. 1:18-22)

All Christians realize very well the fact that Jesus is the personal savior of each individual who accepts Him. What is less well realized is that Jesus is also the savior of the world as the world. He is the savior of the whole world, not only of individuals but of society, of nations. Jesus is the redeemer of the world. Everything in the world must be touched and enobled by the redemption of Christ.

True respect for the name of Jesus means taking one's part in the great work of the Church, the work of applying the redemption of Jesus Christ to everything in the world. Our Lord has given each of us a name, the name of Christian. This name indicates the role we are to play in His plan of salvation for the world. It is the Christian who carries Christ into the home where he lives, the office or plant where he works, the tavern in which he meets his neighbors and friends, the community organization in which he works with his fellow citizens. Our Lord gave the example and the teaching. He also gives the grace to help His followers to do His work in the world. But He relies on the members of His Church to be Christ wherever they are and in this way to Christianize the world in which they live. Only if the followers of Jesus take part in this apostolic work can they be said to have the respect of His name which should characterize them.

application: If we are to carry the name—that is, the teachings—of Jesus Christ into the world, we must do two things. We must know these teachings. It is not enough to coast on the catechism we learned long ago in school. We must learn the teachings of Christ in their application to modern society as the Church teaches them to us in the papal encyclicals. A modern Catholic who can read and has not read *"Mater et Magistra"* and *"Pacem in Terris"* is surely guilty of neglect. His thinking can hardly be what it should be as a follower of Christ in the mid-twentieth century. Secondly, we must get to have the mind and heart of Jesus Christ by opening our hearts as we read of Him in the Scriptures. We must come to think and to feel about people, whether they be bus riders in Mississippi or Indians in Peru or the people next door, as Jesus Christ thinks about them and feels about them.

FEAST OF THE HOLY FAMILY

CHRISTIAN CHARITY IN THE HOME

aim: To show that the family is the school in which love for others is learned and developed.

suggested introduction: The Mass for the Feast of the Holy Family teaches the importance of love in the Christian family.

development: 1. It is within the family that human beings learn to live as human beings, and Christians learn to live as Christians.

2. In the first Scripture reading from the Mass of the Feast of the Holy Family, St. Paul gives advice which fits Christian family living very well.

3. The ordinary civil behavior and good manners which people show in daily life should be, for the Christian, a manifestation of Christian charity, and should be practiced in the home as well as outside of it.

application: Everyone might very profitably read again the words of St. Paul in this morning's Epistle and apply them to himself.

Background for Development:

introduction: In the Mass of the Feast of the Holy Family the Church prays to Christ, who "sanctified home life with untold virtues by being subject to Mary and Joseph," asking Him to assist us to imitate the example of the Holy Family. (Cf. Collect from the Mass of the Feast of the Holy Family).

By being born into a human family, our Lord emphasized the importance of the family as the school in which men learn to live together in harmony and in love. St. Luke says that Jesus went back to Nazareth and "advanced in wisdom and age and grace before God and man" (Luke 2:52). Our Lord grew and developed and learned naturally, in a normal, human way. Therefore He learned courtesy and manners and all the amenities of life in the home of Joseph and Mary at Nazareth. Here, as in everything else, Jesus gives us the example which all men are to follow.

1. The family is, in a sense, the world in miniature. Within the family the interdependence which is so evident among human beings is also present. The family has also been called the Church in miniature. It is within the family that, according to God's wise plan, human beings learn to live as human beings and Christians learn to live as Christians. The virtues which mark a mature Christian are inculcated, fostered and developed in the home. The old adage, "charity begins at home" is literally true. Love for others, respect, reverence for the person, kindness and consideration—all these qualities which are necessary for a civilized person, let alone a Christian, begin at home.

2. This is the truth which the Church teaches us in the Mass of the Holy Family. She gives us the words of St. Paul, referring to the way Christians are to live together, and applies them to the family, showing us how the members of a Christian family are to live together in harmony and love. In the first Scripture reading of this Mass we find a selection from St. Paul's letter to the Colossians:

"Brethren: put on, as God's chosen ones, holy and beloved, a heart of mercy, kindness, humility, meekness, patience. Bear with one another and forgive one another, if anyone has a grievance against any other; even as the Lord has forgiven you, so also do you forgive. But above all these things have charity, which is the bond of perfection. And may the peace of Christ reign in your hearts; unto that peace, indeed, you were called in one body. Show yourselves thankful. Let the word of Christ dwell in you abundantly: in all wisdom teach and admonish one another. . . ." (Col. 3:12-16).

There is hardly a word here which does not describe how the members of a Christian family live together. They are, indeed, God's chosen ones, a "little Mystical Body," filled with the divine life of Christ, with the Holy Spirit dwelling within them. Nevertheless, they are human. They have their faults and shortcomings. Some in the family must exercise authority. Others are subject to authority. For all the situations which will occur they need the advice of St. Paul. They need a heart of mercy, kindness, humility, meekness, patience. They need God's help to "bear with one another" and to "forgive one another if anyone has a grievance against any other." They must all make a great effort to practice charity if the peace of Christ is to reign among them in their home.

3. All men know that it is necessary to be civil and polite in everyday life. They know that it is necessary to be decent to people, to display good manners, to practice patience, to control one's temper and to try to be good humored. People could not hold their jobs if they did not act this way. It is sad to see, however, how some people shed their good manners when they are back at home with the family. There is, of course, a more relaxed and informal air in the home, but the

courtesy and consideration and politeness which characterize people at work and at school surely ought to be evident in the home as well. It is strange to think that people are habitually kind and courteous to those whom they do not even know or at least do not know very well, and thoughtless and unkind to the only ones who would genuinely and sincerely mourn them if they died tomorrow, the members of their immediate family.

Christians should realize that what others consider merely good manners and decent, civilized behavior should actually be manifestations of charity towards one's neighbor. Saying "please" and "thank you," being kind and courteous and patient are small but very real indications of the reverence and regard we must have for others as children of God. Therefore, these things are necessary not only as a matter of enlightened self-interest, as in the case of good manners on the job, but also in themselves, as part of Christian behavior. A realization of this fact should help members of families to show the same courtesy in the home that they show in other places. Parents should realize that in giving example of good manners and in teaching them to their children they are really fostering the development of Christian virtue. They should give the children Christian motives for practicing courtesy and consideration for others.

application: Everyone, parents and children, might profitably take another look at the words of St. Paul in the Epistle which was read in the Mass this morning and see how they apply in each individual case as regards behavior in the home.

SECOND SUNDAY AFTER EPIPHANY

LOVE AND AUTHORITY

aim: To explain that the exercise of authority by the man of the house is one of the ways by which he shows his love for his wife and children.

suggested introduction: St. Paul's admonition to wives to be subject to their husbands, and the application of this admonition to the modern scene.

development: 1. Authority is essential to a happy home; without it the family cannot function properly.

2. The exercise of authority is a manifestation of the love a man has for his family. It places great responsibility on the man.

application: Fathers and husbands should ask God's help in making decisions. They should ask for help to make these decisions solely out of concern for their wives and children, not for selfish reasons. Wives should cooperate and help their husbands fulfill their role as head of the family.

Background for Development:

introduction: In the wedding Mass the Church reads to the newly married couple the words of St. Paul, "Let wives be subject to their husbands as to the Lord, because a husband is head of the wife, just as Christ is head of the Church. . . . Just as the Church is subject to Christ, so also let wives be to their husbands in all things" (Epistle from Nuptial Mass—Ephes. 5:21-24).

Do these words of St. Paul still apply today as they did in the past? Years ago it was clearly defined what were the duties of husbands and wife. The husband was the wage-earner. The wife took care of the home and did the housework, the cooking and the shopping. Nowadays husbands are to be seen in the super-market, helping with the shopping or even doing it by themselves. Husbands as well as wives can be found in a laundromat. Many wives have entered into the husband's domain by working to help support the family. Husbands, in turn, are assisting in work which was once looked upon as that of the wife exclusively.

There is no doubt that the ways of family life and the things that people do in family life have changed much in the United States, especially since the First World War. This is particularly true in what family experts call the "roles" that the husband and the wife fulfill in the family. Now that most men work only a forty hour week and have much greater use of labor-saving machinery, now that women have greater education, social status, and competence, there has been a great sharing in tasks and prerogatives that used to belong exclusively to men or to women.

So, men wash dishes and women chauffer the youngsters about. So, women are responsible for seeing that certain bills are paid and men are responsible for broiling the steak in the cook-out. So, before any important decisions are made, the pros and cons of the possible choices are discussed frankly and openly.

1. Yet in the happy, well-organized American family of the twentieth century with all of its democratic characteristics, the essential admonition of Saint Paul has not been discarded. In these families the head of the house is the husband, who offers it responsible leadership and stability, especially in times of difficulty and stress. The wife and children obey and respect him, and he consecrates his abilities and

strength to their protection and growth. Authority is not abandoned by the husband, it is merely exercised differently.

For authority is essential to a happy home. Without it, the family never achieves the levels of accomplishments that are open to it. Quarrels, blunders, personal recrimination, lack of achievement, and failure mark the family that lacks authoritative leadership. The family is a society and, like every society, cannot function unless its inner drives are given focus and aim through the decision and stability of a responsible authority. It is the father who is fitted by his very nature to exercise this authority. God made man psychologically and physically suited for this kind of responsibility.

2. This focusing of authority in the man of the house, however, is a responsibility and not merely a reward for having been born a man. True authority makes more demands of its bearer than it does of its subjects. St. Paul told men to exercise authority with the love that Christ himself had for his Church. "Husbands, love your wives just as Christ also loved the Church and delivered Himself up for her. . . . He who loves his own wife loves himself."

True authority is unselfish. The true father thinks first of the happiness of his wife and children and only then of himself. The man who spends the family income, sets up the family schedule or gives jobs to individuals in the light of his own desires rather than the good of others is abusing authority and is a tyrant.

True authority is understanding and kind. Some men confuse power with violence and authority with harshness. Violence and harshness may force momentary acquiescence before greater strength, but they do not win the true obedience of love which spontaneously and generously tries to carry out the will of the superior. The lasting effect of kind authority is cooperation; the lasting effect of harsh authority is resentment. The firmness and stability in the necessary wise use of authority does not imply hardness of heart, anger at every frustration, harsh impatience with others' difficulties and failings.

The wise use of authority in the modern American home is not an easy thing. To get each member of the family to do his best, to guide the youngsters toward a desire for a full life, to balance tolerance with firmness, to achieve the long-range goals dispite the individual failures, to love each individual with his own difficulties and peculiarities, and to get all to cooperate in mutual love for each other and for the family—to do all of this with humility, patience, and the ever-present knowledge of his own limited ability and goodness is what is asked of each husband and father.

It is not strange that failure and mediocrity here are frequent, for spiritual blindness and selfishness are common among us. It is clear why authority cannot be regarded as the tool of a man's comfort and prestige. It is rather his peculiarity and heavy responsibility. It is the badge of his manhood—the symbol of the fact that he has put aside the irresponsibilities of adolescence. It is the extension of Christ's authority in his life over the little ones whom Christ loves so much. In their lives, he is another Christ whom they obey because his love for them is so strong that he would "deliver himself up for them."

application: The sacrament of Marriage gives special graces to enable husband and wife to fulfill the role which is theirs in the family. We should ask God for these graces. When a husband and father must make a serious decision he should seek God's help in making it, asking for guidance to know whether he is acting out of selfish motives or out of concern for his wife and children. He should examine his conscience on the right use of his authority as head of the family when he goes to confession. Wives should help their husbands to fulfill their role as head of the family. They should stick by the decisions of the husband as head of the family. They should be extremely careful to "build the father up" in the estimation of the children by their example and their word.

THIRD SUNDAY AFTER EPIPHANY

THE HOLINESS OF PARENTS

aim: To show that parents have a special obligation to be holy so that they can form Christ in their children.

N.B.—This sermon should be carefully compared with the one for next Sunday. Here, the necessity of holiness for parents is treated; next Sunday the point will be specific Christian attitudes which parents should have and should try to develop in their children.

suggested introduction: The scene in which Jesus sets a child in the midst of His disciples and warns of the gravity of scandalizing a child—Matth. 18:1-8.

development: 1. Parents, more than anyone else, are the ones who, by their example, form their children and give them their sense of values.

2. In order to form Christ in their children, as they are bound to do, parents must be Christ-like themselves.

application: Parents show their love of their children by good example. Parents should receive the sacraments of

43

Penance and Holy Eucharist frequently, weekly if possible, to obtain
the special graces they need to become holy.

Background for Development:

introduction: One day some of the disciples of
Jesus came to Him with a question as to who was the greatest in the
kingdom of heaven. Our Lord replied by calling a little child to Himself. Holding the child before the disciples, Jesus said to them, "Amen
I say to you, unless you turn and become like little children, you will
not enter into the kingdom of heaven. Whoever, therefore, humbles
himself as this little child, he is the greatest in the kingdom of heaven."
Then our Lord spoke these words, which should give serious pause
to anyone who has a hand in the rearing or training of children, ". . .
Whoever causes one of these little ones who believe in me to sin, it
were better for him to have a great millstone hung around his neck,
and to be drowned in the depths of the sea. Woe to the world because
of scandals! For it must needs be that scandals come, but woe to the
man through whom scandal does come!" (Cf. Matth. 18:1-8).

These words, coming from the lips of the gentle and merciful Savior,
are strong words indeed. Our Lord has a heart full of love and mercy
for sinners, but, in His love for the young and innocent, He reminds
us of the punishment which God will mete out to anyone who gives
scandal to children.

1. One of the great facts which modern psychology teaches is the
utter importance of the early training of children. The earliest years,
the pre-school years, are the most important. What the child sees,
hears and learns during these years will have the most profound effect
on his future development. There is a very important point here for
parents. It is they, almost exclusively, who influence the child during
these crucial years. The sisters and the priests will come into the
child's life later on, but during these earlier, even more important years
it will be the parents who affect him. The story is told of a young
mother who asked a child psychologist when she should begin to train
her child. "How old is the child?" the expert asked. "Two months,"
replied the mother. "Hurry home as fast as you can," the doctor said.
"You are two months late already." Whether or not this story exaggerates
it does make a good point: even before a child is able to talk, even
before he appears to understand what is going on about him, he is
receiving impressions, he is being influenced, he is being molded and
formed.

No one is in a better position to give good or bad example to a
child than his or her parents. To begin with, no one else is so important
to the small child. Besides, no one else is so continually on the scene.

Nuns and priests can be on their best behavior before the children. They are not with them day and night. Parents have to be themselves; they are on parade at all times.

A child learns by imitating those whom he loves and by growing in the experience and in the approval which he receives. His learning usually involves the hero he admires or the villain he despises. In his admiration of the hero, he tries to be as much like him as possible. He walks, talks, dresses and views life in the way his hero does. However much parents might wish it otherwise, in dealing with children our actions speak so loudly that they do not hear the words we say.

Therefore, the example which the parents set before their children is a very critical element in their growth in virtue and in the love of God. The parents hold the first place in their children's lives. For a small child, they are almost its total world and experience. Therefore the things which parents do become the only things the little ones can absorb and imitate.

If parents really love their children they will realize that example, not the material things of this life, is the most important thing they can give their children.

2. Studies have shown that people who go to church, whatever their religion, are as a general rule children of parents who went to church. Religious habits are formed in the home. There are some exceptions, of course, but any sister or priest knows the story from experience in parishes. All Catholic schools put great emphasis on assistance at Mass on Sunday and at least weekly Communion. In parishes where parents are indifferent it is the same sad story year after year. The children attend Mass and receive Communion Sunday after Sunday during the school year. Yet despite all the teaching and preaching given in the school, attendance drops off very sharply in the summer, and after graduation from grammar school the majority come back into the pattern set by their parents. Those who continue to receive Communion frequently are, as a rule, those whose parents receive Communion frequently.

Attitudes toward religion and the Church are acquired in the home. Children whose parents exhibit real faith, faith which is not ashamed to show itself in prayer and in application to daily life, are apt to develop a strong faith themselves. Children whose parents speak respectfully of the hierarchy and the clergy and the sisters are apt to have a sense of respect and reverence themselves.

There are Catholics whose aspirations and ideals are not at all Catholic. They value money and pleasure and social position as the greatest goods. They are really living for this world, regarding eternity as something which can be attended to later. Their attitude toward religion is legalistic. They miss the whole spirit of Christianity. Parents who are of this type can hardly fail to transmit their attitude to their children. On the other hand, parents who are truly Catholic, who understand the meaning of the Christian life, whose values are truly Christian and who are actually striving to live a Christian life, can hardly fail to give their children a Christian attitude toward life.

application: The matter of reception of the sacraments is important in the question of holiness of parents. Christian parents have a special sacrament through which Christ acts in them, giving them grace to live up to the duties of the married state and become holy. But the sacrament of Marriage was not intended to exist in a vacuum. Our Lord expects parents to use the sacraments of Penance and the Eucharist, too, if they are to grow in holiness with the sacrament of Marriage. Parents should receive the Eucharist every time they offer Mass and use the sacrament of Penance often both for their own spiritual growth and in order to give example to their children.

FOURTH SUNDAY AFTER EPIPHANY

CHRISTIAN ATTITUDES AND THE CHRISTIAN FAMILY

aim: To show that Christian attitudes are to be acquired in the home.

suggested introduction: The behavior of children during recent school integrations reflected the attitudes of parents.

development: 1. The home is the most potent influence in implanting attitudes.

2. Children learn their attitudes on politics, race, law and order, sex, marriage, education, etc., from their parents.

application: Parents who love their children must try to give them the proper Christian attitudes on these subjects.

Background for Development:

introduction: When school opened one year there were the usual disturbances over the integration of certain schools. A news-magazine carried two pictures of the first day in two recently integrated schools. In one picture a Negro and a white child were quietly playing together. In the other a little eight year old boy was screaming curses at the Negro children and holding a sign telling them to go home. The caption was simple, but it told a profound truth. It stated that children imitate their parents. In the first school the adults had prepared for and accepted integration. In the second the parents were demonstrating and protesting against integration. The sermon last week stressed that children imitate the religious habits and attitudes of their parents, who must be holy in order to form the proper religious attitudes and habits in their children. This basic idea that the responsibility parents have to form proper attitudes and ideals in their children is so important that it can be repeated this week with a different application.

1. We Americans put great emphasis on the school. We rely a great deal on the school. It is even sometimes assumed that the school is the greatest factor in molding and training a child and giving him his formation for life. Actually—and this in no way detracts from the importance of the school—the strongest influence in the life of a child and the one which gives him his orientation to life, is the home he comes from. It is the parents and the attitudes of the parents which have the most to do with shaping the attitudes of children. Everyone who has anything to do with schools can testify that it is extremely difficult to overcome the influence of a bad home environment and that it is easy and gratifying to work with children who come from a good home. This is simply evidence of the truth of the Church's teaching that the parents are the ones who have the primacy and principal right and duty of educating the child. It is within the family, according to God's plan, that children receive their basic formation and training for life.

2. It is amusing to observe every four years during a Presidential election the attitude of grammar school children toward the candidates. Some of them wear campaign buttons. They are quick to cheer for the candidate their parents favor and are apt to boo the man their parents oppose. This phenomenon cannot be dismissed as a bit of childish foolishness. Political analyists say that more than 80 per cent of the people in the country usually vote the way their parents voted. This means that a small percentage of the voters, the swing voters, control the destiny of the nation. If this analysis is accurate it points up the obligation of parents to give their children good reasons why they favor one party over the other, so that the children later in life will vote not from instinct but from a political philosophy.

A Christian attitude toward race is another important attitude which must be implanted, first of all, in the home. Here is an area in which parents have a tremendous responsibility, since one of the greatest scandals of our age is the scandal of racial prejudice among Christians. A Catholic would sin against faith were he to believe that any race is by nature inferior to others. He would sin against justice by denying human rights to another. He would sin against charity by refusing to love, with a practical and effective love, all men, of every race. These principles must be instilled in children in the home, long before they are to be taught in school. The Christian family is the school in which children should first learn that all men are to be thought of and treated as God's children, that all men are to be treated as Christ Himself.

Anti-semitism and dislike of the Negro are passed on from parent to child, even in Catholic families, by the use of derogatory nick names and by the broad sweeping statements which apply the sins of an individual or a small group to the entire group. Parents have a special obligation to avoid the use of such words and statements in their home. Otherwise they will scandalize their children.

In all fields of life this cause and effect relationship between parents' and childrens' attitudes is apaprent. In some areas in large cities 70% of high school students drop out of school before graduation. While in the suburbs of the city only 10 per cent drop out. One of the major factors in this drop out rate is the attitude of the parents toward school. In one area the parents feel that school is a waste of time, since no matter how much education you have, other factors such as color or race will keep you from getting ahead. In the suburbs, parents know the value of education. Therefore their children not only finsh high school but also try to go to college.

The attitude of parents toward sex and the size of the family, toward the observance of law, toward honesty in business, toward any subject you can mention is reflected in the attitudes of their children. There are exceptions, it is true, but in general children will have the same attitude as their parents.

application: Parents have a grave obligation to love their children and to help their children become well formed Christians. Husbands and wives would do well to have a quiet discussion on which attitudes they might improve in their homes.

THE CHRISTIAN FAMILY IN MODERN SOCIETY

aim: To point out that the pagan and secular society in which we live affects Christian families, and to urge parents to react in an apostolic way.

suggested introduction: The story of Robinson Crusoe intrigues us because it presents a situation so different from our own. No individual or family lives in isolation from society.

development: 1. The Christian family lives in society and is profoundly affected by it. Today that society is, at best, pagan.

2. This situation provides a challenge to Christian families. Only one of three possible responses is worthy of a Christian—to penetrate the pagan culture and change it.

3. The job of re-Christianizing family life cannot be done in isolation. Families need support from one another.

application: Two organizations which are of immense value to families in helping them to help both themselves and other families are the Christian Family Movement and Cana Conference. Married couples who are interested in doing real apostolic work in the family apostolate as well as in revitalizing their own family life should investigate the Christian Family Movement. All married couples should take advantage of the opportunity which their parish offers in providing "Cana Days."

Background for Development:

introduction: Everyone is intrigued by the story of Robinson Crusoe. It is fascinating to consider the adventures of a man who had to forge a life for himself on a desert island, cut off from civilization. One of the reasons such a story is fascinating is that it is so alien to the experience of people, so completely different from their own lives. We live in community with our fellow men, both as individuals and as families. If Robinson Crusoe had been a father, who brought his wife and children with him to his desert island, his problems would have been greater. His family would have been deprived of the institutions of society which serve their educational, recreational and medical services. There would be no books, no newspapers, no magazines, no radio or T.V. There would be no give and take with other families. Here would be an example of something which does not happen—a family which is uninfluenced by other families and by the culture of a civilization.

1. The Christian family lives in a society. It does not live in a vacuum. And it is profoundly affected by the society in which it lives. The Christian family today lives in a society which is at best pagan, if not actively anti-Christian. Here we do not have the aggressive attempts of society to stamp our religion and Christian values from the lives of people. American parents do not have to meet in the basement at night with their children to teach them religion and try to give an antidote to the poison which was injected into them at school and at youth organization meetings. But the pagan influence is all around us, nevertheless. The standards of those who provide movies and T.V. programs are not Christian standards. The advertizing with which we are continually bombarded is materialistic and worldly and gives a false picture of life. The Christian family today is a minority group in a predominantly pagan culture. Our secular society accepts without question practices which are opposed to Christian principles. Birth control, divorce, race prejudice, the cult of pleasure, concern only for the good life in this world—these are only examples. The importance of parental attitudes in shaping those of their children has been stressed. But every Christian parent knows how difficult it is to inculcate Christian attitudes in the face of the pressure of the society in which we live.

2. This situation proivdes a challenge to Christian families. How does the Christian family respond? Basically, it can respond in any of three ways:

a) It can yield to the pagan culture. Sadly, the family can go along with the stream; it can be overcome by secular pressures. It can give up the struggle to the extent that members of Catholic families are indistinguishable from their pagan neighbors. Their opinions, judgments, attitudes and actions are shot through with secularism.

b) It can withdraw from the struggle. The family can attempt to retreat, to pretend that there is no outside world which affects it. It can seal itself up in a "family ghetto" where it jealously guards its Catholic heritage. This solution is most unrealistic, since we cannot isolate ourselves in this highly complex society. There are too many entrances to the outside world. We must mingle with our pagan neighbors every day. We work with them; we shop with them; our children play with their children and may attend school with them; we serve on committees with them; we exchange ideas with them in conversation. If we are not engulfed by the pagan world, we are surely surrounded by it. We cannot go off like St. Simon Stylites and live on a pillar in the desert. We cannot live like a hermit in the middle of the block Withdrawal is impossible.

c) It can *penetrate* the pagan culture. This is the only course worthy of a Christian. The task of the Christian is to leaven the mass, to take the offensive, to bring Christian principles to bear on society. Rather than yield to or withdraw from a pagan attitude, the job of a Christian is to change it. If a social institution is shot through with corruption, it must be reformed along Christian lines.

For the family this means more than carrying on a holding action. Certainly the family must maintain its values and principles; it can never compromise them. Christian parents must stand firm against the argument, "But everybody else is allowed to do it." They must always uphold the sanctity of marriage and family life in the face of bad example all around. But beyond this it must present to society an image of solid Christian living. It must open the doors of its home and let people see what it is that makes this family different. It must act on the environment so that other families can more easily live a Christian life. It must interest itself in the problems which affect families in the neighborhood, in the city, in the nation, in the world.

3. This job of re-Christianizing family life cannot be done in isolation. Families need support, not only from their Catholic teaching and institutions, but also from one another. Thus the need for Catholic families to join together in groups which are designed not only to preserve Christian family values, but also to prepare family people to penetrate society, to train them solidly, so that they will become the salt of the earth, giving flavor to society.

application: The Cana Conference is an organization which seeks to help married people achieve the optimum of happiness and holiness in their marriage. It provides many services for married couples as well as for those who are preparing for marriage. The "Cana Day" provides an opportunity for married couples to gain a greater insight into each other and their marriage. All married couples should make a "Cana Day" every year when the opportunity presents itself.

The Christian Family Movement is a specialized movement of the lay apostolate for married couples. It aims at helping all families. Through this movement many married couples have found real spiritual growth and the great satisfaction and fulfillment which comes from taking part in the Church's apostolate. Information about the Christian Family Movement is easy to obtain. A few interested and a priest willing to act as chaplain are all that are needed to start this movement in a parish.

THE PROBLEM OF SEPARATION AND DIVORCE

aim: To point out the growing evil of divorce and broken homes and to review the procedure and legislation in this matter.

suggested introduction: One of the greatest offenses against charity today is the tragedy of divorce and separation which is growing every day.

development: 1. Divorce is a social problem as well as a religious problem.

2. Catholics may not separate or seek a civil divorce at will. They are bound by the laws of God and of the Church.

3. The procedure to be followed in the case of marriage problems.

Background for Development:

introduction: One of the greatest offenses against charity towards individuals and also toward the common body of society and especially the Mystical Body of Christ is the tragedy of divorce and separation that seems to be mounting in our day. Statistics on divorce are terrifying. A few years ago California had almost two divorces for every three marriages. Informed sociologists tell us that if the present trend continues, we will have a national divorce rate of one divorce for every two marriages within twenty years.

1. Too many people believe that this problem is purely a religious one, and in so doing they make a big mistake. It certainly is religious; it involves charity in its very fundamental nature. Catholics, of course, have courage to oppose divorce on religious grounds. But we must be charitable to our neighbors by enlightening them that the law of God demands their cooperation as well. Moreover, the mere idea of good neighborliness demands their cooperation.

Our newspapers lament the spread of juvenile delinquency and look for its cause. The cause is precisely in the broken marriages. The children are delinquent because their parents are delinquent. In too many cases, parents are fighting shy of their obligations. Instead of regarding parenthood as a priceless privilege, they regard it as a burden. Our boarding schools and institutions under the supervision of Charities are overcrowded because parents do not want to take care of their children.

2. Catholic people who are married must live together until they have obtained permission from lawfully established Church authority to live separated and apart. This rule is contained in the Code of Canon Law. The Council of Baltimore forbade Catholics to approach the civil courts for a divorce or separate maintenance without the permission of the Bishop of the Diocese. Those who would defy this rule were to be punished by the Bishop of the Diocese. Those who would defy this rule were to be punished by the Bishop with Church penalties. The Church in her deep concern for her children has two big considerations in view:

A.   The moral dangers for a married person who lives separated from his or her spouse. At first glance people might fail to see such dangers. However, taking human nature at its face value, we know that even apparently innocent companionships end up in deep affection and attraction. Married people have become accustomed to companionship. If they do not find it in married life, there is a great temptation to seek it elsewhere. Too many good Catholics are persuaded that such associations are licit so long as nothing immoral happens. Wise in her experience, the Church knows how many souls have been lost from friendships that started innocently. For this reason, she strives with all her efforts to keep married people together.

B.   Scandal: The individual lives of Catholics can be great in promoting the common good and in avoiding scandal. Catholics are always a measure in the eyes of others. In the religion we profess, we make strong claims. Many outside of the fold are anxious to see how well we fulfill these claims in our lives. Our Blessed Lord bade us to let our light shine before all men. He intended that this light should glorify God and give an example to others. Certainly Catholics flocking to divorce courts are a tremendous puzzle to non-Catholics and a terrible example to their own brethren.

The only reason admitted by the Law of the Church, wherein Catholics on their own authority may separate from their spouse, is the reason of adultery on the part of their spouse. The adultery must be certain and not merely surmised. The innocent party must not have given permission for such a thing or caused it. And should the innocent party condone it afterwards, he forfeits his right to separate.

There are other reasons, of course, why difficulties come into marital life. There are reasons, at times, for separation. In all of these instances, the permission of the Bishop of the diocese must be obtained before Catholics may go to see lawyers and become engaged in suits in the civil courts.

3. People having marital difficulties are, first of all, to see the parish priest before they take any other step. The parish priest will guide and counsel them to the best of his ability and endeavor to work out their problem. They should see him on several occasions.

If the parish priest cannot succeed in his efforts to reconcile these people, then he will fill out a special case history and submit this to the office of the Bishop, the Separation Court of the Archdiocese. From these requests, sent by the parish priest, the parties involved will be given a special appointment in the office of the Separation Court or in the office of the Catholic Family Consultation Service. They will be invited to discuss their problems with marriage counselors or with priests who will give them the necessary permission to go to the civil courts.

The decision of the Court is binding in conscience. Anyone who would disobey the command of the Court would be guilty of a sin of external disobedience to the Bishop of the diocese. By such disobedience he renders himself unworthy to frequent the Sacraments.

Catholic lawyers who would represent a client in the civil courts without the necessary permission of the Bishop would be committing a grave sin of disobedience. A principle for a laweyr is that he may do licitly what the client does licitly. Any lawyer who would resort to subterfuge in giving the case to another lawyer to handle is just as guilty as if he handled it himself, because he is cooperating in the great evil of divorce.

application: Catholics should understand the teaching of the Church on marriage and divorce. Many people outside the Church have false ideas about what the Church teaches on this subject. Some think the law against divorce and re-marriage is merely a Church law, like the law of Friday abstinence. Many others do not see the reasons behind what they consider to be the Church's undue strictness in this matter. Catholics should, by their word and their example, show others what the Church's attitude towards marriage is.

LENT AND EASTER

QUINQUAGESIMA SUNDAY

LENT AND PENANCE

aim: To show that the whole Church prays and does penance during Lent and that our Lenten observance is a sign of our love for one another.

suggested introduction: The scene which took place outside the Church before Mass on Sundays in the days when public penance was required for certain sins.

development: 1. It is the whole Church which does penance during Lent.

2. Our Lenten observance is an act of love for our fellow-Catholics.

application: The whole Church is being strengthened and purified during Lent. If we assist at Mass every morning during Lent, we should do so with the realization that we are praying for all our brothers and sisters in the faith. We should have this fact before our eyes as we fast and perform the special penance we have decided to do. We might also select one or two specific individuals who particularly need spiritual help, and do penance for them this Lent.

Background for Development:

introduction: In the ancient Church, in the days when public sinners were obliged to do public penance for their sins, a strange scene would take place on the Sundays of Lent outside the church as the time of Mass approached. At the door of the church stood the public penitents. They were dressed in sack-cloth. They stood quietly with eyes downcast as the people passed through the entrance into the church. But they spoke to the people who passed them, asking their prayers. And the people looked at them with sympathy and understanding. Every now and then someone would pause, put out his hand to a penitent, murmur a word of encouragement, give a promise of prayer. There was a bond between the ordinary faithful and those who were doing public penance during the forty days of Lent. All realized that on Holy Thursday the penitents would receive absolution and would rejoin the congregation of the faithful for the celebration of the Eucharist. During the difficult time of penance all were aware that they were united by the bond of love, which showed itself in prayer for one another.

1. The penitential aspect of the forty days of Lent arose from the practice of public penance which was done during this period. At first only the repentant public sinners did penance during this time. Later, as the practice of public penance died out, the forty days of Lent came to have a more general significance. The whole Church came to view this time from Ash Wednesday to Easter as a time of penance, a period of purification in preparation for the annual celebration of the great feast of Christ's Resurrection. All the faithful adopted the practice of receiving ashes on Ash Wednesday as a sign that they were entering upon a period of penance, whereas formerly only the public penitents

had ashes imposed on them. The change was significant. It meant that the Church as a whole was doing penance during Lent.

Most people view Lent in an individualistic sense. They see it as a time when they ought to do penance for their own sins. They fail to see any communal aspect in Lent. Yet the Collect of the Mass for the First Sunday of Lent states that it is the whole Church which is doing penance during Lent, the whole Church which is being purified:

"O God, each year you purify your Church through the lenten observance. May the good works of your Church obtain for us the grace we ask for through our self-denial."

The individual aspect is there, of course. Each person is to do penance for his own sins. But this is only part of the story. As members of the Mystical Body, we are never alone. We rejoice together; we suffer together; we pray together; we do penance together. The Church imposes the lenten fast on all those who are able to keep it. Those who are keeping the fast are keeping it for the whole Church, not only for themselves.

All Catholics feel that they should do some special penance during Lent, over and above the official penance which the Church imposes in the lenten fast. The Church urges all the faithful, children as well as adults, to do so. What is asked is threefold—prayer, fasting and almsgiving.

2. It is important to realize the fact that we do penance during Lent as members of the Mystical Body. First of all, such a realization brings home the conection between penance and fraternal charity. If we fast and do penance as members of the Church, we are doing it for one another. This is an important point for everyone to realize. It is more meaningful to do penance when one realizes that it is not a negative thing but an act of love. It is hard to make a sacrifice. It becomes easier when we are making one for another person. Furthermore, many good people, and perhaps most children, do not really see why they should do a great deal of penance. This is not pride or presumption. It is true that they are not great sinners. Actually they do not need to do much penance for their own sins. It makes a great difference to these people when they are told that they should do penance during Lent for others. A child may have difficulty seeing why he should give up his favorite television program in order to do penance for his little faults and peccadillos. He will find it much easier to do this act of penance if he realizes that he is doing it for someone who has been away from the sacraments for years or someone who is in danger of dying unrepentant. Adults, too, will find it more meaningful. They will come to see Lent as a time when they express very concretely their love for their fellow members of the Mystical Body.

The Church is a living body. In any living body all the parts are affected when there is sickness or infection in one part. The whole body goes to work to stop the infection. The body temperature rises, white corpuscles multiply, new substances are manufactured and carried to the seat of the infection. So it is with the Church. The strong members come to the aid of the weak and ailing members, those whose faith is weak, those who are living in sin, those who are careless about Mass and the sacraments. The saints have always been aware of this great fact. They did great acts of penance, much more than was necessary for their own sins. They did penance for sinners, for those who refused to do it for themselves. When the Cure of Ars became pastor in that little village he was appalled to find that his people were worldly and materialistic. They did no penance. The saint's reaction was immediate—if his people would not do penance he would do it for them. His prayers and fastings are well known. Well known, too, is the effect that the Cure's penance had on the souls of his people.

application: The spirit of love should be the keynote of our Lenten observance this year. First of all, we should consciously do the penance we do for others, for all our fellow members of the Mystical Body, and especially for those who will not themselves do penance this Lent. We should pray for others more often than usual this Lent, for our fellow Catholics, for our separated brethren, for those of other faiths, for those who have no religion, offering our penance for them also. All who can do so should try to offer Mass daily during Lent. Nothing unites us so much and provides so much mutual help as the Eucharist.

Explain the Lenten Regulations

FIRST SUNDAY OF LENT

EVERY CATHOLIC IS A MISSIONARY

aim: To show that all Catholics must manifest their love for people who do not have the faith, by being missionary minded.

suggested introduction: Our Lord expressed the Church's mission and the part all must play in it when He said, "The fields are already ripe for the harvest. And he who reaps receives a wage and gathers fruit unto life everlasting, so that the sower and the reaper may rejoice together" (Cf. John 4:34-38).

development: 1. The population of the world is increasing amazingly, thus increasing the preponderance of non-Christians over Christians. Everywhere the Church has a gigantic task.

2. All Catholics must be fired wtih the missionary spirit.

application: (Next Sunday will be Mission Sunday). Each must respond. All can contribute money and prayers. Some can heed Christ's call to give all or part of their lives as workers in the missions.

Background for Development:

introduction: Jesus was seated beside Jacob's well in Samaria. The Samaritan woman to whom He spoke of living water had just departed. The Apostles had just returned from town, where they had gone to buy food. Jesus pointed to the wheatfield a few yards away. "Lift up your eyes," He told the Apostles, "and behold the fields are already ripe for the harvest. And he who reaps receives a wage, and gathers fruit unto life everlasting, so that the sower and the reaper may rejoice together" (John 4:35-36).

One sows, another reaps, but it is the one work of Christ which is to be done by all—the work of bringing Christ to all men, everywhere in the world. "Go into the *whole world,*" our Lord told the Apostles, "and preach the Gospel *to every creature*" (Mark 16:16). The Church's work is worldwide. Its object is every single man, woman, and child in the world. Its agents are every single member of the Church.

1. In some places in the United States it is easy to get the impression that Catholics make up a large percentage of the general population. It is necessary to see the world picture. It is amazing to learn that from 1910 till 1960 more people were born into the world than were born from the time of Christ until 1910. In other words, in that half century from 1910 till 1960 there probably were more eople alive on earth than had lived all through the first 19 centuries after Christ. This increase is mounting every year.

Of all these growing millions of people less than one out of five is baptized a Christian. Furthermore, non-Christian peoples are growing faster than we are. Mohammedans, for instance, are increasing about four times faster than Catholics.

In our own country, North Carolina is less than 1% Catholic, while Tanganyika is 16%. Georgia is 1½% Catholic; the Congo is 33%. Even a city like Chicago which has a Catholic population of 2,000,000, only 5% of the 900,000 Negroes in the city are Catholic. In other words, right here in our own country, too, we have truly missionary territory.

These are the facts—grim as they are. And yet we hear the words of our Lord ringing in our ears—for Jesus had compassion on the crowds!

"They are like sheep without a shepherd" (Mark 6:34).—"They shall hear my voice and there shall be one fold and one shepherd" (John 10:16).—"Going therefore teach all nations" (Matt. 28:19). What is to be done?

2. The Popes have given the answer. All Catholics must be fired with a great missionary spirit. This missionary spirit is a spirit of love for those who do not know Christ. It prompts us to do all we can to help them know the Lord. Pope Pius XI insisted that Catholics in mission territory help convert the non-Catholics. Today we see thousands of native sisters, brothers, priests, bishops, and even several Cardinals, working in the mission field, which encompasses nearly 2/3 of the world's population. Pius XII and John XXIII have insisted on lay mission workers, pleading for the layman to assume his full role in the missionary work of the Church. All over the world, laymen are answering—doctors and nurses, teachers and catechists, social workers, carpenters and plumbers. Everywhere, more and more, year after year, they are serving side by side with missionary priests and sisters, each doing his proper job in the work of Christ's Church.

Some time ago a young lady who is a medical missionary in Vietnam was interviewed by a leading magazine. "Did you take any vows as a lay missionary?" "Certainly," she answered, "my baptismal vows." In other words, she pointed out that every Catholic by the vows of his baptism, and by the grace of Confirmation must be a missionary in one way or another. Pope John insisted on this point. Many young people have heard his voice and volunteered a year or more of their lives as Papal Volunteers for the mission needs of Latin America and even more are serving as Extension Volunteers in the home missions of our own country. The United States calls on its young men to give several years in military service. It challenges generous men and women to serve in the Peace Corps. Certainly Christ in His Church has a prior claim on our lives.

Now and then we American Catholics get the idea that we are expected to staff and support the missions single handed. Actually, our record is not that impressive. Tiny Holland, for instance, has nearly three times as many priests in the missions as we do. Ireland has more than twice as many. While our financial support has been much better, the average American Catholic still does not give one dollar a year to the missions.

application: (Next Sunday will be Mission Sunday once again). Surely there will be many students who will hear our Lord's invitation to a dedicated life in the missions. There will be other men and women in our churches who could give a year or more of their lives as a lay mission worker. They should pray and consult their confessor. The U.S. Hierarchy has initiated a program to recruit lay workers for the home missions. This is the Extension Volunteer program which is under the direction of the Catholic Extension Society. This year over 200 men and women, mostly recent college graduates, are at work in the south and south-west under this program. Most of the work involves staffing schools, teaching catechism, taking census, and doing social work.

We too must make our sacrifice in answer to that same call. We must pray and we must give to the collection for the missions (which will be taken up next Sunday). And it must be a sacrifice. We are members of Christ, Whose whole life could be summed up in that one word "sacrifice." We are members of Christ, "Who gave himself for us" (Tit. 2:14).

SECOND SUNDAY OF LENT

THE MEANING OF HOLY THURSDAY

aim: To prepare for Holy Thursday by showing how the Last Supper was the fulfillment of the Passover, the celebration of the Old Covenant, in the celebration of the New Covenant in Christ's blood.

suggested introduction: The Last Supper began as the celebration of the Passover ritual. Jesus then fulfilled the Passover by inaugurating the new offering of the Covenant in His blood.

development: 1. The rite of the Old Covenant gave place to the far more wonderful rite of the New Covenant in Christ's blood, the Eucharist.

2. The bond of the New Covenant is the love which unites us all in Christ. The Eucharist both symbolizes and effects our union in Christ.

3. The celebration of Holy Thursday is a special celebration of the anniversary of the Last Supper.

application: All who can do so should arrange to be present at the evening Mass on Holy Thursday and to make a special preparation for it during lent.

Background for Development:

introduction: A few days before the feast of the Passover, the Apostles came to Jesus and asked Him where He was planning to celebrate the Passover meal with them that year. It was our Lord's practice to celebrate this ritual each year, as did all good Jews. During His public life, He celebrated it with His "family," the Apostles. As the Apostles prepared for what would prove to be their last celebration of the Passover, the Last Supper, they were expecting nothing more than the familiar, traditional ritual meal in which they took part every year on the feast. And, as a matter of fact, the Last Supper began as the traditional Paschal meal always did. Jesus invoked a blessing on the ceremonial wine. Each took a cup of wine and drank it. There followed the washing ceremony, accompanied by prayer. Next came the bitter herbs, dipped in the juice of dates and raisins mingled with vinegar, then a second ceremonial cup of wine. Then, very likely, John, as the youngest member of the "family" asked Jesus, who acted as the father, the traditional question. "Father, what do you mean by this service?" To which our Lord would have replied, "It is the passover-sacrifice to the Lord, who passed by the houses of the Israelites in Egypt, when He struck down the Egyptians, but spared our houses." The Paschal meal then proceeded according to the prescribed ritual, until, near the end of the meal Jesus fulfilled this age old sacred rite in the Eucharist.

1. In the mind of the Apostles the Last Supper was to be simply the Passover meal. It was the solemn commemoration of the great events in the history of God's people—the Exodus from Egypt and the making of the Covenant at the foot of Mt. Sinai. The Passover recalled that the Israelites were bound to God by the great Covenant their ancestors had entered into with God. God would be their special protector and would cherish them "as the apple of His eye." They would worship God alone, shunning false gods, and would show their faith in God and their love for Him by keeping the Mosaic Law, which was the bond of the Covenant. The Passover feast recalled with great joy the bond which united God and His people.

In the mind of Jesus the Last Supper was to be much more than the celebration of the traditional Passover ritual. It was to be the fulfillment of that rite. It was to be the celebration of a new Covenant, a far greater Covenant which God would make with all men through Christ on Calvary. "I have greatly desired to eat this passover with you," Jesus told the Apostles, "before I suffer." The connection between the Eucharistic offering which Christ made as He fulfilled the Passover at the Last Supper and the offering He made of Himself on the Cross was essential. Christ offered Himself liturgically at the Last Supper in anticipation of the offering He would make of Himself on the Cross. It is the same sacrificial offering. It is the sealing of the new Covenant, a Covenant which is sealed not in the blood of animals, as was the one made at the foot of Mt. Sinai, but with the most precious blood of Jesus Christ. "This is my blood of the new covenant," Jesus said at the Last Supper, "which is being shed for many" (Mark 14:24).

"All ancient rites give way to the new," says St. Thomas. The rite of the old Covenant gives place to the far more wonderful rite of the new Covenant. The Passover yields to the Eucharist, the shadow to the full reality, the symbolic paschal lamb, to the Lamb of God, whose blood was shed for all mankind. And that blood is the new bond which binds the members of Christ to God and to one another far more wonderfully than the Law of the Covenant bound God's people in the Old Testament. The celebration of the Eucharist is the continual renewal of the New Covenant in Christ's blood which binds us together ever more closely in a union of love. "This is my body which shall be given up for you; do this in remembrance of Me.... This cup is the new Covenant in My blood; do this as often as you drink it, in remembrance of Me. For as often as you shall eat this bread and drink the cup you proclaim the death of the Lord, until He comes" (1 Cor. 11:24-27).

2. It is within the setting of the Last Supper that our Lord gave us His new commandment, the commandment to love one another as He has loved us. The conection is of the greatest importance. The Holy Spirit teaches us that the Eucharist, "the proclamation of the death of the Lord until He comes," is the celebration of the new Covenant of love. The bond of that Covenant is the love which unites all the members of Christ's Mystical Body, the Spirit of Love who dwells within and who gives and increases the gift of charity in Christ's members. The Eucharist binds us together in love ever more closely. It both symbolizes the unity which we have for one another in Christ and effects that unity.

3. Every Mass, every celebration of the Eucharist, is a renewal of the Last Supper, a renewal of the new Covenant of love in the blood of Christ. But every year on Holy Thursday we celebrate the anniversary of the Last Supper in a very special way. We do so only after having gone through a spiritual renewal during the forty days of preparation which the Church gives us in the season of Lent. In ancient times, Holy Thursday was the day of the great reconciliation and reunion. The public penitents, who had been excluded from the community of the faithful at Mass all during Lent, were absolved from their sins on that day and admitted once more to the congregation of the faithful in the celebration of the Eucharist on Holy Thursday.

The whole Christian community celebrated the Eucharist on that day with special love and fervor, recalling that it is the Eucharist which binds us ever more closely together in love.

application: Before the reform of the Holy Week liturgy only a relatively few members of the parish came together to offer Mass and receive Communion on Holy Thursday. Communion was distributed outside of Mass throughout the early morning. The one Mass of the day was offered in the morning, with the children present and those few adults, mostly housewives, who could be on hand at that time. Now, with the restoration of the Holy Thursday liturgy, the parish Mass is celebrated in the evening, when most of the people can be present. Mass is permitted in the morning in order to allow the children to receive Holy Communion. But the great Mass which brings the people of the parish together in love and union on this great feast of unity is the parish Mass in the evening. Everyone should be present at Mass on Holy Thursday and should receive Communion with special devotion.

BISHOPS' RELIEF FUND

THE BISHOPS' RELIEF FUND COLLECTION

aim: To show the work done by the Bishops' Relief Fund and to urge the people to contribute generously to its collection (next Sunday).

suggested introduction: In the magazines we read we often come across a picture of a pathetic child, suffering from poverty and hunger. We think, rather vaguely, that we ought to do something about the situation.

development: 1. The Bishops' Relief Fund is a means by which we can show our Christ-like love for those who are less fortunate than we.

2. All over the world there are people who are helped by the aid we give through the Bishops' Relief Service.

application: We can heed Christ's plea, which He makes through His suffering members, by contributing to the collection for the Bishops' Relief Fund (next Sunday).

Background for Development:

introduction: As we turn the pages of a magazine, we often come upon a picture of a pathetic child—big eyes staring, with an expression of sadness which seems doubly out of place in the eyes of a child, a ragged, pitiful creature who is sick from hunger and poverty. Underneath the picture in the magazine is the address of a relief agency and an appeal. As we look at the picture, we sigh and think that we ought to do something. But the organization is one we have never contributed to; it is unfamiliar to us. We turn the page rather regretfully and go on about our business.

The child pictured in appeals like this is only one of millions. And there is something very definite and concrete that we can do about the situation, through an organization which is familiar to all of us.

1. For the past twenty years or so, the Catholics of America have harkened to the appeal of their Bishops to contribute to the aid of their needy brethren all over the world. The Catholic Bishops' Relief Fund is the means by which we can show our Christ-like love for those who are less fortunate than we are.

The Catholic Relief Services represent the largest organized voluntary effort ever made to assuage human suffering on an international scale. The Services depend upon the single once-a-year collection taken in the parishes on their behalf.

People do not know what they provide when they give to the Bishops' Relief Fund. Last year almost 2 million tons of relief supplies were sent to 80 countries all over the globe. The value of these shipments totaled almost 200 million dollars. The supplies reached some 40 million people.

But the enormous figures and statistics cannot tell the whole story. They cannot show the gratitude in the eyes of a child for clothing sent by the Catholic Relief Services; they cannot show the contented smile on the face of the old woman who has eaten her first full meal in months with the food the Relief Service has sent.

2. It is better to look at people than at statistics, the people who are suffering from want, the people who desperately need the help which the Catholic Relief Services can give them.

We remember Korea as the scene of international conflict. But, to a poor worker in the rice paddies like Mr. Sung, war, communism and democracy are all just empty-sounding words. All Sung can think about is the feeding of his family. He has three children, and his parents and his wife's father also live in his small hut. He has to work 16 hours a day in the rice fields to provide them with just the bare minimum sustenance. His three children are all under seven years of age, and when the cold, bitter Korean winter sets in, they will not have enough warm clothes to protect them—unless someone helps them. Mr. Sung and his family must rely on the Catholic Relief Services.

Pedro is four years old. He lives in Porto Alegre, Brazil. His mother is dead and his father has to provide for Pedro and his two sisters with his meager earnings as a fisherman. Pedro spends most of his days, unlike other lads his age, just sitting outside the broken-down shack he must call home. He does not play, because most of the time he does not have the energy to take part in the games most boys his age play. Pedro is hungry. If he is very lucky, he eats one full meal a week. Pedro desperately needs help if he is to survive.

Mr. Sung and Pedro are not alone in their misery. There are many others. In Latin America alone there are millions who need food and housing. The young and emerging nations of Africa face problems far beyond their own capacity to solve. There are the destitute of India and Pakistan, whose major problem is simple nourishment—the victims of hurricanes, earthquakes, flood and famine in Iraq, Iran and Japan—the exiles from Cuba who need homes, food, clothing, jobs, a new start—the millions of hungry and homeless everywhere. These are our brothers and sisters in Christ.

Pope John XXIII has told us to remember these people. "Make them alive and close to your hearts," the good Pope pleaded. "Think of them with love and wish for them all the blessings and comforts that God has given you. We ask you to make extra sacrifices during the holy season of Lent. Personal, voluntary sacrifice must mark the life of every follower of Christ. We can make sacrifices by denying ourselves, by offering to God, and to others in His name, some desired good or possession."

application: We should count our many blessings—and share them. God has seen fit to allow us to live in the world's "country of plenty." We must share our plentiful bounty with those who need it more than we do.

And who are these people? Who are the Mr. Sungs and the Pedros? These "least of my brethren" are Christ Himself in the distressing disguise of need. When we help them, we help Him.

"I was hungry—and you gave me to eat.

I was thirsty—and you gave me to drink.

I was naked—and you covered me."

We can answer Christ's plea by contributing generously to the Bishops' Relief Fund collection (next Sunday).

THE MEANING OF GOOD FRIDAY

aim: To explain the Good Friday services and encourage the people to take part in them.

suggested introduction: A description of the Good Friday services in Jerusalem in the fourth century.

development: 1. The veneration of the cross gradually developed into its present form. While the people are venerating the cross the choir is singing the reproaches.

application: All Catholics should take part in the Good Friday services and receive Communion on that day.

Background for Development:

introduction: About the year 385 A.D. a pious pilgrim named Etheria wrote an account of her journey to the Holy Land. Her description of the Good Friday services in Jerusalem helps us to understand our present Good Friday services.

Etheria reported that on Holy Thursday everyone went to Mass at 7 p.m., received Communion and then went home for a meal. After supper the people gathered at the Mount of Olives to commemorate the Agony in the Garden with hymns, readings and prayers. About midnight they went to the place where our Lord was taken prisoner. There the Gospel of His capture was read to them and the whole crowd broke into loud lamentations. They stayed in the garden till morning, when they returned to Calvary where the Passion of the Lord was read to them. Sometime in the forenoon the relic of the true Cross was venerated. The ceremony was simple. It took place at Calvary. The bishop sat on his throne. Before him was placed a table covered with a white cloth on which was the relic of the true Cross. The clergy and the laity came forward and kissed the wood of the Cross.

At noon the people assembled again on Calvary to listen to readings from scripture, to pray and to sing hymns. The liturgy ended at 3:00, the time of the death of the Lord.

1. The ceremony of the veneration of the cross spread to other cities in which there was a relic of the true Cross. In the seventh century it reached Rome, where a large segment of the true Cross was kept at the Church of the Holy Cross. As time went on other ceremonies, taken from the Eastern Liturgies, were added. The "Hagios O Theos," in which the Church hails the crucified Lord as her God is first sung

in Greek, then in Latin, showing that this part of the ceremony came from the Byzantine Liturgy. The reproaches which the Church puts in the mouth of the Savior came from the Greek, most probably from the Syrian Liturgy.

The veneration of the cross, in the earliest times, was not part of the liturgy of Good Friday. It was held, as we have seen, before the three hour service in the afternoon. Later it was incorporated into the services which are composed of three parts, 1) Readings from Scripture and prayers for all people; 2) the veneration of the Cross; 3) Communion.

After the prayers for all classes of people, the priest takes off his cope and stands facing the people at the foot of the altar on the Epistle side. All the crosses in the Church have been veiled since Passion Sunday. Now, to focus the attention of the people on the awesome moment of Jesus' Crucifixion, the priest unveils the cross in three stages. In an ascending key he sings three times, "Behold the wood of the Cross, upon which hung the salvation of the world." The people respond, "Come, let us adore." The cross is taken from the priest and held by two acolytes on the altar platform, and a candle placed on each side. The priest and his assistants approach the altar with three genuflections and kiss the cross. Then the cross is taken to the altar rail and the people come up and kiss it. Our kiss is a sign of our contrition and our love.

While the veneration of the cross is taking place the choir is singing a series of antiphons called the "Improperia" or reproaches. These are reproaches uttered by Jesus against the faithless people to whom He had given so much. He reminds the people of the great benefits He gave them in the Old Law, and then chides them for their ingratitude. His cry, "My people, my people, what have I done against you, or in what have I offended you? Answer me," should cut to the heart, reminding us that our Lord has given us so much and we have been so ungrateful. He even asks in this beautiful prayer, "What more should I have done to thee and have not done?" He tells how He delivered the people from slavery in Egypt and they prepared a cross for Him. He planted Israel as His vineyard and they gave Him vinegar to drink. He destroyed the first born of the Egyptians and His people delivered Him up to be scourged. He led them out of Egypt, and they turned Him over to the chief priests. He opened the sea for them, and they opened His side with a spear. He led them through the desert by a pillar of cloud, and they led Him to Pilate. He fed them with manna in the desert, and they beat Him. He struck down the kings of Canaan, and they struck Him on His head. He gave a royal sceptre to Israel, and they gave Him a crown of thorns. He raised the people to great heights and they raised Him on the cross. We must realize that these reproaches are really directed to us. God was good to the Israelites, but He has been even better to us. For every one of the gifts He gave them, He has given us many more. If He reproaches the Jews for their faithlessness, how much more does He reproach the faithless Christian, the one who is living in sin? Good Friday commemorates the passion and death of Jesus, but it does so in order to stir up the spirit of repentance in our hearts.

Between the sections of the Reproaches there is an ancient chant which praises Christ as God, "Holy God, Holy Strong One, Holy Immortal One! Have mercy on us!" The rite ends with a joyful song of praise to the cross, "Your Cross, Lord, we adore! We praise and acclaim Your holy Resurrection. Behold, through the wood of the Cross joy has come in the whole world."

application: Everyone should participate in the Good Friday services. We should unite ourselves with Jesus and realize that His sufferings were for us. We should show by our participation that we are sorry that our sins have caused Him to suffer and die. We should show our love by being united to one another and to Christ in Holy Communion on Good Friday.

FIRST PASSION SUNDAY

THE MEANING OF HOLY SATURDAY

aim: To encourage the people to attend the Easter Vigil service.

suggested introduction: The liturgy is like a family meal, in which all should participate.

development: 1. When the communal nature of the liturgy was lost sight of, the people became silent spectators.

2. The first step in liturgical reform was to establish the new order of the Holy Week services.

3. In the Easter Vigil service Christ brings us into contact with His resurrection.

application: All should take part in the Easter Vigil this year.

Background for Development:

introduction: A family meal is usually a raucous affair. Baby is pounding on the table; younger children are playing with their food and demanding attention; older children are talking all at once. On special occasions, when the fine china and silverware are out and when guests are present, the children are more subdued. In most homes, however, where there are a number of children, the dinner hour is not the time to soothe the parents' jangled nerves. Many people long for a peaceful and quiet dinner hour, but they realize that much of the family *esprit de corps,* much of the family give-and-take, much of the family's exchange of ideas and information would be lost if everyone had to eat in silence while a trained reader read poetry or a string quartet played dinner music.

The Mass is the family meal of the Christian community. When Catholics come to Mass they are a family gathering at home to honor their Father. They are not an audience going to a theater to be entertained. Catholics at Mass should take an active part in the Mass. They should say or sing these prayers which properly belong to the congregation. There should be dignity and beauty in the Mass, but no one should expect the congregation to give a faultless and perfect performance, such as is given by well trained altar boys and a well rehearsed choir.

1. This basic idea that the Mass and the liturgical services of the Church are not only the actions of the priest but also the actions of the people was lost sight of for many centuries. The liturgy was seen, not as the homage of children gathered to praise their Father, but as the homage paid to the divine King by the official members of His royal court. Majesty, dignity, pomp, display and beauty were emphasized to the detriment of participation. Because the liturgy was looked upon as the exclusive work of the priests, strange things happened. For example, the most important Mass of the year was celebrated at a time when most people could not attend it. The services which preceded that Mass were usually performed in the presence of a handful of people by a priest and a few altar boys. This was the Easter Vigil service, which was celebrated early on Holy Saturday morning.

2. Things have changed now. Guardini says that we live in an age in which "the Church is coming to life in the hearts of men."

One of the most significant manifestations of this coming to life, this revitalization has been the changes which the Holy See has begun to make in the liturgy. The first major change was the establishment of the new order for Holy Week services. This new order was not adopted for ascetical reasons; it was adopted for pastoral reasons. Its aim was to make it possible once more for the people to participate in the Holy

Week services. The times of the services were made more flexible so that they would be more convenient. Participation was urged. Services were shortened. The most important service of the year, the Easter Vigil, was put back where it belonged. If possible, the services are to start on Holy Saturday night at such an hour that the Easter Mass will be celebrated about midnight on Easter Sunday. The Easter Mass is the most important Mass of the year. At one time Easter was the only feast day. Each Sunday was looked upon as a little Easter. It is true that most Catholics go to Mass on Easter day, but the Easter Vigil is the Easter celebration in all its fullness.

3. Pope Pius XII said, "The liturgical year is no cold and lifeless representation of past events. Rather, it is Christ Himself, living in His Church. . . . This He does in order to bring the souls of men into contact with His mysteries and so make them live by them." In other words, when we attend the Easter Vigil service we should not expect to have a great and moving emotional experience; we should not expect to be thrilled by fine music, but we should expect to open our hearts to the mysterious action of Christ by which He will pour into our souls the great benefits of His death and resurrection. Christ did not live and die for us, and then put all His grace into a reservoir from which the Church could dole it out to people. Christ Himself, acting through His Church, passes out these graces to us. When we are baptized, it is Christ who gives us the divine life and removes sin. It is Christ who forgives us our sins in the confessional. It is Jesus who offers this very Mass in which we are participating. True, He does these things through the actions of the priest, but nevertheless, it is He who does them. So too, with the feasts of the Church. In them through the solemn actions of the Church Christ brings into the lives of His children the graces He first won for them 2,000 years ago. To celebrate Easter properly and to obtain all the graces we can from this feast we should participate in the Easter Vigil service which prepares us for the feast.

At the Vigil service Jesus, through the ceremony of the blessing of the new fire and the Easter candle, gives us the grace to appreciate Him as the Light of the World, who has come to dispel the darkness of sin and error. Through the reading of the prophecies and the singing of the Exultet He helps us to appreciate better the great work of salvation which He began after the fall of Adam and Eve. If there is a baptism at the Vigil service, Jesus comes to the ones who are baptized to give them new life. Then He arouses in us all a deeper sense of our dignity and duties as Christians as we renew our baptismal vows. Finally, in the Mass, our Lord renews His death and resurrection and comes to feed us with His body and blood.

application: Many Catholics have yet to take part in the Easter Vigil service. This is an unfortunate state of affairs.

Many more come to Midnight Mass at Christmas. Yet, the Vigil service and the Mass which follows it at Easter is far more meaningful than the Midnight Mass at Christmas. The Easter Vigil provides a real religious experience. It penetrates the whole person, giving a deeper realization of the great and central truth of our faith. It is an incomparable preparation for the celebration of our Easter Mass. Everyone should resolve right now to be present for the Vigil service this year and to participate fully in it.

SECOND PASSION SUNDAY

Read the Passion of Our Lord according to St. Matthew

EASTER SUNDAY

THE PEACE OF EASTER

aim: To explain some of the conditions Pope Pius XII indicated as necessary if peace is to come to the world.

suggested introduction: Christ appeared to the Apostles on Easter and wished them peace.

development: 1. Christ is the Prince of Peace.
2. There is no real peace in the world today.

3. Pope Pius XII outlined five essential conditions which must exist in the world before we can hope for peace.

application: First, we must be at peace with God. Then we must do all we can to establish the social and economic conditions which are conducive to peace. We must back up the efforts of our government to promote programs which coincide with the points outlined by Pope Pius XII.

Background for Development:

introduction: On the first Easter the Apostles were gathered in the Cenacle not far from the cave where Christ was buried. To say the least they were confused. They knew that Christ had died and had been buried. Yet some of the women from their band claimed that an angel had told them that He was alive and risen from the dead. Peter and John had gone off to investigate and had found the tomb to be empty. John recorded his reaction to this discovery in these words, "For as yet they did not understand the scriptures, that he must rise from the dead. The disciples, therefore, went away again to their home wondering . . . at what had come to pass." Suddenly the Lord stood in the midst of the Apostles, even though the door was closed and locked. They cowered in fear. His greeting was simple, "Peace be to you."

1. In this greeting our Lord summed up all that He wanted for men. He wanted them to be at peace with God, with themselves and with each other. He was the Man of Peace. When the prophet Isaias spoke of the Son of David, who was to come and sit on the throne of Juda he said, "For a child is born to us, a son is given us; Thy name is . . . Prince of Peace. His dominion is vast and forever peaceful." The angels took up this cry when they proclaimed to the shepherds in the fields that David's son was indeed born in Bethlehem. "Glory to God in the highest and peace on earth to men of good will." Peace has always been associated with Christ. Pope Pius XII said, "Our Redeemer stood forth, the Herald and Ambassador of peace, and in the words of St. Paul, 'He preached the gospel of peace.' "

Even though vicious wars have been fought by Christians since the time of Christ, even though Christian nations are now arming for war, Christ's message of peace has not been lost, nor has the peace He came to bring been destroyed. The fruit of the Lord's death on the Cross is peace. By shedding His blood and conquering sin and death He has made it possible for men to be at peace with God and with themselves. All the people who were at odds with God because of their sins and who have been restored to the friendship of God by the sacrament of penance in the last few days are benefitting by the peace Christ came to bring. They did not go to confession simply because they thought it was time for them to be straightened out with God. They went because the Prince of Peace called them by His actual grace to come and make peace with their Father. All those who receive the Lord in Communion today will be closer to true peace within themselves because, as St. Paul says so simply, "Christ is our peace."

2. But Christ wants us to be at peace with each other also. As we look around the world, we wonder where His peace is to be found. If the prophet Jeremiah were to come back and walk the earth again, he would cry out as he did 2,500 years ago, "Peace, Peace, and there was no peace." In 1939 just before World War II broke out, Pope Pius XII said, "For in every part of the world we see great numbers of men greatly disturbed, anxious as to their fate, tormented with fearful misgivings that seem to hint at still more frightful things to come." Can we, twenty-six years later, say that things are any better or must we conclude as we look around us that "a fearsome anxiety possesses the souls of men?"

3. Pope Pius XII, back in 1939, outlined five conditions which are essential for international order so that peoples might live in a just and lasting peace. We Catholics should keep these conditions in mind whenever we discuss peace. Peace will not come merely from disarmament or from banning the bomb. It will come only when men live together in such a manner that peace is possible. The Pope said that:

1) Big and powerful nations have to respect the right of small nations to political freedom, to economic development, to adequate protection, and to neutrality if such they choose.

2) All nations must respect the rights of minorities, within their boundaries, to their own culture and language as well as to their oportunities for economic development.

3) No nation because of cold and calculating egotism may hoard economic resources and materials which are destined by God for the use of all.

4) The arms race must be stopped; the possibility of total war must be eliminated by nations. Pacts between nations must be observed, and nations must be able to deal with one another in trust and confidence once again.

5) Finally, there is no place for persecution of religion and the Church in a world dedicated to peace.

There are signs that some steps are being made to implement these five points of the Pope's program. Small nations and minorities are being persecuted in some places, but in Africa and other parts of the world the small nations are standing on their own feet. In general, the lot of minorities has improved throughout the world. Nations all over the world, not only the United States, are beginning to share technical knowledge and natural resources with other nations. The persecution of the Church goes on in Communist countries, but in most other countries the Church is remarkably free from government persecution and interference.

application: Jesus Christ came to establish peace between God and man. He united God and man by restoring man to friendship with God. The work of Christ, the Prince of Peace, goes on. Through His Church Christ continues to unite men with God. He wills also to unite men with one another in brotherly love. As members of Christ's Church, we must cooperate in Christ's work of peacemaking. We must remain in the love and friendship of God ourselves. We should do whatever we can to bring others back to friendship with God—those, for example, among our relatives and friends who may have been away from the sacraments for a long time. We must see to it, also, that our ideas are in line with the teachings of the popes on the conditions which are necessary for peace among men and nations.

LOW SUNDAY

EACH PERSON SHOULD CONTRIBUTE TO THE COMMUNITY

aim: To show that each member of the community must make his Contribution to the community.

suggested introduction: The story of Jesus and the payment of the temple tax—Matth. 17:23-26.

development: 1. Throughout His whole life, our Lord contributed to the community in which He lived.

2. The first thing that each member of the community must do is to respect the rights of others—in other words, to practice the virtue of justice.

3. The Christian must do more than practice justice; he must serve Christ in his neighbor by doing his job in the community.

application: We should make the Morning Offering every day. This offering can be made more meaningful and more effective if it is made with reference to the work which we shall be doing during the day as our contribution, as a Christian, to Christ in the Community in which we live and work.

Background for Development:

introduction: One day when Jesus and His Apostles were in Capharnaum, those who collected the temple tax approached Peter and asked him whether Jesus was in the habit of paying this tax in accordance with Jewish custom. Our Lord made it plain to Peter, first of all, that as the Master He was actually exempt from this obligation. Nevertheless, He told Peter that He was going to pay the tax in order to give good example. He instructed Peter to go and catch a fish, and that in the mouth of the fish he would find a coin to pay the tax (Cf. Matth. 17:23-26).

St Matthew tells this story in order to bring out the fact that Jesus complied with the customs of Judaism and lived up to the requirements of the Law.

1. Throughout His whole life our Lord did what was expected of a good member of the community in which He lived. At the prescribed time, eight days after His birth, He submitted to circumcision. Forty

days after His birth Mary presented Jesus in the Temple, and made the required offering of turtle doves for His ransom. When He was twelve years old Jesus accompanied His parents to the Temple as He was expected to do. Our Lord complied with the Law and went up to Jerusalem every year for the feast of the Passover. We may be sure, too, that He complied with all the customs of the little community in which He lived at Nazareth. The Gospel tells us that He was subject to Joseph and Mary.

As a youth and a young man Jesus served the people of Nazareth as a carpenter. During His public life He was at the service of the community at all times. He served the people by preaching to them, teaching them the truths about His kingdom. He was tireless in His work of healing the sick. His activity during His ministry in Galilee is summed up by St. Matthew in the words, "And Jesus was going about all Galilee, teaching in their synagogues, and preaching the gospel of the kingdom, and healing every disease and every sickness among the people" (Matth. 4:23). The people themselves expressed the activity of Jesus during these years of His public life, "He has done all things well. He has made both the deaf to hear and the dumb to speak" (Mark 7:37).

2. Man lives in a community with his fellow man. Each man, as a member of the community, is expected to contribute to that community. Each is expected to serve the others in the community according to the talents he has and the kind of work he does. Each is expected to do his part in promoting the good of all, the common good.

The first thing which each member of the Community must do is to respect the rights of others—in other words, to practice the virtue of justice.

First, there is that form of justice which obliges men to pay their bills, to pay just wages, to do their work faithfully and honestly, to refrain from stealing or destroying the property of others. There is also another kind of justice, which is called social justice. Pope John speaks of this type of justice in his encyclical, "Christianity and Social Progress." This is involved in such matters as cooperation between labor and management, between the government and the people, and between the nations of the world.

The practice of justice in its various forms is the first duty of all in the community. This is the most basic and minimal expression of that love which should exist among men, who live in dependence on one another. The first requirement of love is that one gives his fellow man what he has a right to, and respects his rights and his human dignity. The second requirement is that a man does what he can individually and in conjunction with others, to make it possible for all men to live decent, happy, peaceful lives.

3. The Christian must be concerned with more than merely practicing justice in his life and work within the community. His is to be a life of love, a life of service to his fellow man. There are certain jobs and professions which everyone associates with generous and unselfish service. People expect doctors and priests and teachers to give themselves in service for their fellow man. But why should not the same spirit of unselfish service be expected also of businessmen and clerks and carpenters? A Christian must realize that, whatever his job in the community, he does it not merely to earn a living, but also to serve Christ in his fellow man. Such a realization would change a grudging, perfunctory performance of one's job into a meaningful and fulfilling acceptance of one's role in the Mystical Body. St. Paul tells us that within the Church each person has his peculiar function to perform and that he is to perform it as well as he can for the good of the whole Church. By this St. Paul did not mean working for the Church as an usher or a sacristan. He was talking about working for the Church by doing one's daily job in a Christ-like manner. There are bishops and priests and religious within the Church. There are also bus drivers and policemen and housewives and punch-press operators. Each helps to build up the Body of Christ by doing his work as well as he can. Each serves Christ in the Church by serving the people with his particular work. The Christian thereby develops to its fullness the plan whereby God wills that men should love one another within the framework of their mutual dependence.

application: As members of the Mystical Body of Christ we should try to realize that everything we do is important. Every action we perform should be an act of adoration of God and an act of service to others. We can consecrate our daily actions and make them something of great value in God's sight by offering everything we do during the day to God, uniting it to the offering Christ makes in the Mass. We can make such an offering in just a few words in our Morning Offering prayer. We should renew it during the day—at meal times, for example—by just a thought or a word.

SECOND SUNDAY AFTER EASTER

CHARITY AND THE LAW

aim: To show that the observance of civil law is a manifestation of love for our fellow citizens.

suggested introduction: Little boys playing baseball fight and quarrel because they do not realize that each must sacrifice something if they are going to gain the benefits of playing together.

development: 1. Men have a natural instinct to band together and form a communty. By working together in this community they show their love for one another.

2. All communities need laws. The observance of the law is a manifestation of our love for one another.

application: Catholics should have a great respect for the law. They should also promote good laws which will help and protect all members of the community.

Background for Development:

introduction: It is interesting to watch a group of small boys playing baseball. Seldom does a game go the full nine innings. Usually one or the other boy stalks off the field, feeling that he has been cheated in a close call at the base, or angry because he cannot bat or pitch as much as he would like. The boys argue at the top of their lungs about who is to play what position, who is to bat, whether the runner was out etc., etc. If the bystander watches closely enough he will even notice that the boys usually do not know the rules of the game very well. This experience does teach the boys something. Gradually they learn to work together as a team. They learn that if they are to enjoy the game they have to follow the rules and engage in a great deal of give and take.

1. These two ideas—that people have to work together to achieve a common goal, and that they must follow the rules of the game—are the basis of all forms of community. In the civil community, the government, men band together to obtain those things which they cannot obtain for themselves as individuals or as families. Instead of each family hiring guards to protect its possessions, the families of a community band together and form an army, a police force and a fire department. In other words, men band together in a community to help one another. It is only in a community that a man can be truly a man. In order to live in a community a man must not only take; he must also give. The man who lives outside a community, or who lives in a community but seeks only to get without giving is lessened as a man.

Most people are so used to living in civil society that they seldom think of the purpose of the government. Some look upon the government as something separated from themselves, something outside themselves. Others, like the Communists, look upon the government as the absolute master of the people. Still others look upon the government as the enemy of the people. The Christian must realize that the government is really the people of an area pooling their resources to help one another, to promote the good of all. The instinct in men to band together in a community was implanted by God. When men form a government they are following this God-given instinct. But they are also doing more. They are helping one another. They are showing their love for one another. They are protecting the weak from the strong, the simple from the cunning, the honest from the dishonest. By being good citizens, men are following the Lord's command to love one another.

2. A group of men, banded together to achieve a common end, need certain rules and regulations. In civil society we call these regulations laws. To achieve the common good, individuals will have to sacrifice their own selfish interests. The law determines what is the common good and who will have to sacrifice his selfish interests in order to help achieve the common good. The law determines that certain actions must not be done because they harm the common good. The law determines whose rights shall prevail when there is conflict of rights between citizens. A man has a right to listen to and enjoy his radio, but this right has to be limited if he wants to play the radio at 4 A.M., when other men have a right to get some sleep. A man has a right to transport himself from one place to another, but the law restricts that right when he drives a car in such a way as to endanger other men's rights to life and limb. Most of the cases in our civil courts are simply cases in which two parties claim to have a right to something. They have to call upon the people, the court, to settle their dispute. The laws of our country also help us fulfill our obligation to the world community. We must love all men, not only Americans. The law helps our country in its relations with other countries. It also makes it possible for us to share the benefits which God has given us with other peoples who do not have as much as we do. Pope John in "Mater et Magistra" has urged all nations which have much, to share with those who have little. Just as in the city, state and nation those who have the most contribute the most to the common good, so too in the family of nations those who have much must contribute most to the common good of the whole human race.

application: Too many people look upon the law as something to be circumvented whenever possible. They feel that they should keep the law only if there is a possibility that they will be caught and penalized for breaking it. Such an attitude is un-Christian. The Church is the family of God's children in religious matters. The civic community is the family of God's children in secular matters. The faternal charity which is the bond of unity in the Christian community must extend itself to the overall civic community. If this be so, the laws of the civic community, of the civil government, should be readily obeyed in a spirit of fraternal charity. The Christian, far from being an enemy of the law, should be one of its most natural supporters. By keeping the civil laws which are not manifestly unjust or contrary to God's laws we are showing our love for our neighbor. All laws may not be absolutely just; some may be foolish or unwise, but as long as they do not contradict the laws of nature and God, we should observe them as the best efforts of the civic community to establish justice among men.

This idea, of course, means that the Christian has an obligation to see that the legislature makes good laws and that the protection of the laws is extended to all without favor or distinction. Personal service to others, while most important, can never replace the benefits of a well written law that is properly applied to all people. Many groups of people, such as migrant workers or Negroes, need the protection of law when the sense of personal love and justice fails in a community.

THE CATHOLIC CHARITIES
OF THE DIOCESE

aim: To point out that the work of caring for the needy in this Diocese is the work of the whole Church—i.e., all of us—to show the work of the Charities and to urge a generous response to the Charities collection.

suggested introduction: The story of the disciples of St. John the Baptist who approached Jesus asking whether He was the Messiah. Our Lord replied by citing the works of mercy which He was performing (Cf. Matth. 11:1-6).

development: 1. Christ continues to perform His works of mercy now in His Church. We must all take part in this work as members of the Church.

2. Some examples of the work which the Church here is doing through the Charities of the Diocese.

application: Each of us, as members of the Church in this Diocese, should contribute generously to the Charities collection (next Sunday).

Background for Development:

introduction: One day, as our Lord was preaching to the people, two men who had been sent by St. John the Baptist came to Him to ask whether He was the promised Messiah. Jesus answered, "Go and report to John what you have heard and seen: the blind see, the lame walk, the lepers are cleansed, the deaf hear, the dead rise, the poor have the gospel preached to them" (Matth. 11:4-5).

The sign of Christ's presence among men is the works of mercy and of love which He performs. This was true during the lifetime of Jesus on earth; it is true today, as Christ lives and continues to act in the Church, His Mystical Body.

1. The Church is Christ; therefore the Church performs the works of Christ. She takes care of the sick, the handicapped, the homeless, the old, the poor, those who are in trouble. This is not a side issue with the Church; it is part of her work in the world. It is part of the work of the whole Church—which means everyone in the Church. As Christians, each of us must do the works of mercy for those with whom we come in contact everyday. But we must also do them as the only way we can effectively help many who need help. How else can orphans, old people, and others who need institutions to care for them find help except by the combined efforts of all of us—that is, of the Church? This is the reason why the Diocese maintains the organization which is called the Catholic Charities. By means of this organization the Church—i.e, all of us—is able to perform the works of mercy throughout the whole Diocese.

2. The Catholic Charities is just a term to many people. They have only the vaguest idea of the work which this organization performs. It would be most useful to learn some of the things which the Charities do for the needy in this Diocese.

application: Many other dioceses in this country do not have an annual collection in local parishes. Some raise their Catholic Charities funds by door-to-door solicitation. Thousands of volunteer solicitors call on more hundreds of thousands of Catholic families.

This is not necessary in our Diocese. Our once-a-year Catholic Charities collection in all parishes eliminates this costly fund-raising device—and makes each charity dollar go even farther.

Hundreds of priests, nuns, and volunteers donate their valuable time and service to save more hundreds of thousands of dollars.

And the total cost of administration, supervision and planning makes up *less than two per cent* of the Catholic Charities budget.

Each should do his share as part of the Church in this Diocese, doing

Christ's work of mercy, by contributing generously to the Charities collection (next Sunday).

THE MOTHERHOOD OF THE CHURCH AND OF OUR LADY

aim: To recall how God has blessed us with two spiritual mothers, our Mother the Church and our Blessed Mother.

suggested introduction: Mothers' Day has been given a spiritual significance by Catholics, who not only honor their mothers on that day, but pray for them as well.

development: 1. The Church is our Mother in a very real sense.

2. Our Lord in His great love for us has given us His own Mother as our mother.

application: As we honor mothers today, we should thank God especially for our Mother the Church and for our Blessed Mother.

Background for Development:

introduction: There are certain days throughout the year when the lines outside the confessional are longer than usual. There are days when there are more Communions at Mass than usual. These are, as a rule, the big liturgical feasts of the year, the great holy days, like Christmas and Easter. But there is one Sunday during the year which is no religious feast at all—other than Sunday—when more people receive Holy Communion than usual. That Sunday is today, Mothers' Day. Even though, like so many other things in our day, there is a great deal of commercialism connected with this day, a valid and good idea does come through. Everyone feels that it is right to pause and pay tribute to the idea of motherhood itself and to honor our own mothers in a special way. Characteristically, Catholics not only give their mothers flowers or candy on Mothers' Day. They pray for them. They offer Mass for them. They have given a spiritual significance to the day.

This development is a happy one. It is fitting that we make Mothers'

Day something more than a display of commercialism and sentimentality. There is a solid spiritual reason why we should pause and give thanks to God for the love He has shown us in giving us all the love and guidance of mothers. For God has given us besides our natural mother, two spiritual mothers, the Church and our Blessed Mother.

1. Catholics are quite accustomed to speak of the Church as their mother. The phrase "Holy Mother Church" is a consecrated phrase. And yet the motherhood of the Church is often taken for granted without a realization of its full meaning. A real appreciation of the Church as our mother should lead to a greater love for the Church.

The Catholic idea of the Church as our mother is thrown into sharp relief by comparing it with the Protestant idea of the Church. Adherence to the Church for a Protestant is a consequence of the faith which gives a man justification, a necessary consequence, but a consequence. One Protestant writer expresses the Protestant position this way: "For all those who confess their faith in God, belonging, submission and devotion to the Church, the visible body of Christ, are an unavoidable necessity. . . . All those to whom the Holy Spirit gives the certitude of justification cannot persist in their solitude: they are summoned to join themselves with their brothers in the faith, to make up this visible body of which the glorified Christ is the heavenly and invisible Head."

For Catholics, adherence to the Church is not a consequence of a salvation which is already acquired, but this very salvation itself is a consequence of our adherence to the Church. It is not our coming together into one which constitutes the Church. The Church is there before us to give us our re-birth in Christ. Even when Protestants call the Church "mother" it is in a different sense than Catholics do. Protestants say, "The Church is the mother of those of whom God is already the Father." Catholics say, "We have God the Father because the Church has given us the God-life and made us children of God."

The Church is our mother because she has given us the divine life. The baptismal font has been called the womb of the Church. The Church is our mother because, having given us life, she nourishes us in the Eucharist. The Church is our mother because she gathers us together to worship God, our Father. The Church is our mother because she teaches us the eternal truths which God has entrusted to her and prepares us for everlasting life. It is as a loving mother that the Church binds us with her laws. Every one is reasonable. Every one is for our own good. We need to fast, we need to pray. As a good mother, the Church sees to it that we do these things. She never loses interest in our spiritual welfare. She insists that we do the minimum; she encourages us to go on to greater heights. She never loses hope for any of her children, never refuses to forgive no matter how serious or how numerous their sins.

Pius XII described the motherhood of the Church very beautifully: "Oh, the loving Mother is spotless in the sacraments, by which she gives birth to her children and nourishes them, she is spotless in the faith, which she has preserved inviolate always, in her sacred laws imposed on all, in the evangelical counsels which she recommends, in those heavenly gifts and extraordinary graces through which, with inexhaustible fecundity, she generates hosts of martyrs, virgins and confessors.

"But it cannot be laid to her charge if some members fall weak or wounded. In their name she prays to God daily 'Forgive us our trespasses;' and with the brave heart of a mother turns at once to nurse them back to spiritual health" (Encyclical on the Mystical Body).

2. Our Lord has given us His own mother as our mother. This is something that He did not have to do. He might have come into the world wholly miraculously, without a human mother. Instead, He chose and prepared for Himself he who is the greatest of all creatures. But Christ chose Mary not only out of love for her, but also out of love for us. He chose her with the full intention of bequeathing her to us as He died on the cross.

Catholics do not have to be reminded of the motherhood of our Blessed Mother. They know her love, her maternal solicitude, her continual intercession, her great mercy, which follows her children all through their lives. They know how powerful her intercession is. They pray to her with the utmost confidence. What we fail to do, perhaps, is to thank God often enough for having given us Mary as our Mother.

        application: As we honor our natural mothers today, we should offer special thanks to God not only for our earthly mother but also for our Mother the Church and our Blessed Mother.

FIFTH SUNDAY AFTER EASTER

SOCIAL PROBLEMS ARE SOLVED NOT ONLY BY LAWS BUT ALSO BY LOVE

        aim: To show that laws are neecssary to solve many of the social problems which face us today, but that love is also necessary.

suggested introduction: We Americans are concerned with our image in the eyes of foreigners, and so we treat Negroes from Africa as equals. But often the same dignity is denied to an American Negro.

development: 1. Laws are necessary to overcome many of the bad effects of segregation and discrimination.

2. Laws are not enough; Christians must be moved by love to help establish a climate in which the dignity of the Negro is recognized.

3. We must learn this love in our church, where all men of all races must be welcome, and at the altar rail, where all men eat of the body of Christ.

application: A simple application of this principle is to refrain from using derogatory names when referring to Negroes and to teach our children that the use of such words and names is unchristian.

Background for Development:

introduction: The highway between Washington and New York runs through Maryland, and has been a constant source of embarrassment to the United States; colored people are regularly refused service in restaurants, and foreign diplomats in numberless cases have received the same treatment.

A few years ago in Virginia a Nigerian Consul was refused breakfast in a restaurant, and the international indignation which resulted was such that the President of the United States, in a gesture of apology, invited the Nigerian to have breakfast at the White House. The restaurant owner complained that he should have been told that the man was from Nigeria. The Nigerian commented: "Is it any less an insult when it happens to Negro American citizens?"

In Boston at a meeting of the American Committee for UNESCO in 1961, a member of one of the African embassies in Washington, D.C. said that the African delegations in Washington were at the point where one more instance of discrimination suffered by an African leader, whether in housing or in public accommodations, would spark a mass exodus out of Washington on the part of the diplomatic corps of African and Asian countries.

The injustice of discrimination in housing, in schools, in restaurants, in theatres, in hotels, etc. is eroding the reputation of the United States, thus threatening the balance of international power and world peace.

The irony for American Negroes is that Americans have been slow to see the injustice of racial discrimination when suffered by those who have been American citizens for over 300 years. Only the international consequences, not the moral consequences, have stirred us.

Laws are becoming acceptable for international reasons which have been necessary for moral reasons for a long time. Laws are needed to rid our society of discriminatory practices which are as sinful as robbery and murder.

1. Racial discrimination and compulsory racial segregation are sinful because they deny access to opportunities and services which human beings need for a good life. This has been historically the case, as the American bishops pointed out in their pastoral letter of 1959. However, even if faculties and opportunities provided were to be equal, such practices are still sinful, because they withhold something even more important—human recognition and acceptance in the human community where human growth and maturity depend upon fraternity, esteem of one's fellows, and Christian love.

Thus, while laws are necessary, they are not enough. At best, they establish justice, fair treatment, toleration. Even their enactment requires more than a spirit of justice in society. Normally, they are enacted and enforced only when men and women are moved by a fraternal concern for other human beings, their dignity as children of God, their rights as heirs to all that belongs to Christ on earth and in heaven.

2. Laws establish equal opportunity, whether in housing, in employment, or in civil rights. But laws cannot make a person feel wanted, welcome, accepted, equal. This results only from the spirit of love and charity in the souls of Christian men and women, whence it penetrates offices, labor unions, parishes, neighborhoods. Charity seeks the good of others, their growth, their dignity, their development. Charity seeks unity, which always reflects the life of God, unity in the Mystical Body, unity in temporal and secular life.

3. Charity is learned within the life of the Church which, as Pope Pius XII said, is at all times "open to all men without exception." All are welcome, all wanted, no one merely tolerated, no one excluded. To exclude anyone unfairly or racially is also to exclude oneself.

Nothing is a greater threat to the Church's work today than racial prejudice and separateness. It threatens the very essence of the Church, which is not a sect, not a national clan, not a bastion for social clanishness. It is Christ, extending Himself in time and space, needing all men for His completeness, giving all men their highest dignity, their true life, which for all men is life in God. The Church is Catholic, or it is nothing.

The individual parish, each organization and institution of the parish, indeed the heart and mind of every member of the Church, has as its model Christ Himself and the Church as she really is. The parish where all are of one nationality, all of one social class, all of one color is not necessarily the ideal. The ideal parish or organization

85

is the one that shows forth the glory of the Church, overcoming racial, class or nationality biases and actually uniting all men on a higher level, on Christ's level, on God's level.

4. The center of the Catholic life is the altar and the Holy Eucharist —the one bread for all to eat that men might become one bread; the physical body of Jesus Christ, which unites us more closely within His mystical body, His extended Self. It unites by infusing into us the love of God.

application: A simple application of this principle to love can be made to the language we use about minority groups, especially Negroes. If we are motivated by a spirit of love we will not use words which are offensive to them. We will speak of them as Negroes, and we will correct our children anytime they use an offensive word. This is a simple manifestation of love. It is easy enough to do. It is also most important. We cannot have the love of Christ for a man to whom we may apply contemptible names.

ASCENSION THURSDAY

THE ASCENSION OF OUR LORD

aim: Christ's Ascension is an integral part of our redemption, not just the finale to His eventful life.

suggested introduction: The sacrifices of the Old Law prefigured man's longing for the Ascension and the glorious reconciliation of man with God.

development: 1. The mystery of Christ's Ascension is inseparable from His death and Resurrection.

2. The Ascension is an event of deep personal meaning to each of us.

application: To be a follower of Christ means to live a life transfigured with an awareness and a confidence of the dignity of our calling, to sacrifice ourselves that we may rise in Christ and stand with Him before the Father. To be a follower of Christ in this way means to be the happiest of men, for it means to live by faith in the certainty that one has overcome the most agonizing problem of human life—death. It means to be a child who has at last found the way to reach his Father. It means to rejoice on this feast of the

Church, remembering the Ascension of Our Lord, and to look forward to our own.

Background for Development:

introduction: Throughout their long history there developed in the heart of the chosen people an intense longing for God. With faith they struggled to meet the demands of this longing, to bridge the infinite distance between themselves and their Lord. Nowhere did this drive take such clear and poignant form as in their sacrifices. Much more than the superstitious motions of the pagans to ward off the displeasure of some superhuman force, these were the forceful expressions of a children's need to communicate with their Father. And so out of the darkness of the Old Testament they kindled fires on their altars, and their priests plunged their offerings into the flames. The people sang the praise of God as the sacrificial fires consumed ox and lamb and incense. With the smoke trailing heavenwards, they hoped in their hearts that somehow they were reaching the invisible God they worshipped and recognized as their own. Because of the faith with which this was done, God accepted its meaning. But it was to remain until the Ascension of Christ an incomplete gesture. It was done more in the hope than in the realization that man could really reach the heavenly Father. As the Jews watched the wistful trails of smoke streak the sky above their holy city they must have wondered how they would ever follow the sacrifices they had sent to heaven as feeble symbols of themselves. The answer came clear when the angel of the Lord spoke to the Apostles on Mount Olivet and asked: "Men of Galilee, why do you stand looking up into the sky?" No longer shall men look into the sky and wonder. It is the Ascension of Christ that must fill them with the confidence that what He, the first of all men, had done they and all who were to be His followers would also do. The question of the Jews was answered; their longing now fulfilled.

1. Christ's Ascension is an integral part, the completion, of His Sacrifice and our Redemption. We must not think of this final mystery of Our Savior's life as a mere finale simply added to the eventful days and years that preceded it. It is more than the Bible's happy ending to be told after the suffering of His death and the shock of His Resurrection. It is more than a magnificent farewell to the Apostles, prepared for the end of Our Lord's earthly career. It is not at all something added. It is one with Our Lord's death and Resurrection. It is one in the plan of the Heavenly Father: His will was that His Only-begotten Son should die for the sins of mankind, rise to express His victory over death and sin, and ascend to express the reconciliation

of mankind with the Father, thus making clear and complete the meaning of our redemption. It is one in the mind of Christ Himself: He embraced His death to express His union with us, to share in the lot of our suffering; He embraced the mystery of His Resurrection to fill us with life and courage again; He finally embraced the closely related mystery of His Ascension to show us our way to the Father through Himself, the way in which our life in Him would endure forever. A close bond of meaning unites these three mysteries and makes them one. We cannot treat anyone as incidental without losing the meaning of each, nor without disturbing the balance of our own lives as Christians. For if we practically lay all the emphasis on the death of Our Lord, our imitation of Him will be more a way of dying than of living. We will strive to follow Him in suffering, in observing the laws He and His Church impose. But our hearts will be dulled, and the joy He would want us to experience in our faith will be diminished. Being a Catholic will seem to us mainly a matter of bearing trials and resisting temptations. Hardships and laws will so preoccupy us that we will not see beyond them to what they lead to. We will not see them clearly as the necessary step to a happiness that surpasses any happiness that man could know, a happiness that should begin even now, in this life. It is this happiness that should keep us from being legalistic or formalized in the practice of our religion. As dear to us as is the image of the crucified Lord, we must not fail to remember Him also as the glorious Lord, reigning in Heaven. He was one with us in His death only that we might be one with Him in His Resurrection and Ascension.

2. The Ascension of the Lord is an event of deep personal meaning to each of us. It is, first of all, something in which each of us takes part. For just as Christ died for us all, so He ascended into Heaven, in the name of us all. His flesh and blood are the same as ours. It is this flesh and blood that He offered in Sacrifice. The flesh and blood that He immolated, that was glorified by the fire of the Holy Spirit, that He gave over to God, was our flesh and blood. It was not therefore Himself alone, but the whole human race that Christ offered to the Father in the pledge of undying worship, and He sent it up to heaven. It is in the mystery of His Ascension that mankind bridged the infinite gap between itself and God. In His Ascension the longing man had expressed on the altars of the Jewish people was at last fulfilled. In the Ascension of Christ man had at last found something of himself that he could send to God.

application: As we celebrate the Ascension of Our Lord, mindful of His triumph over sin and death, a triumph in which we all share, we should be impressed anew with the fact that our religion is a joyful thing. So often the impression is given that being a Catholic is a joyless matter of laws to be obeyed and restrictions to be accepted. This negative, legalistic spirit is utterly alien to the true spirit of Catholicism. One of the ways in which we take part in the apostolate of the Church is to show others our attitude that our religion is a thing of joy. Even in the midst of suffering, we are one with the risen Christ who sits at the right hand of the Father in heaven, who has gone to prepare a place for us.

SUNDAY AFTER ASCENSION

THE ROLE OF GOVERNMENT IN DAILY LIFE

aim: To teach that public authorities must take an active interest in all things which further social progress for the benefit of all citizens.

suggested introduction: The federal government's laws and regulations influence every field of our daily life.

development: 1. The government is not the master of the people; rather, it exists to serve the people.

2. Catholic social teaching tells us that intervention by the government in business and daily affairs of people is sometimes necessary.

application: Each citizen must determine when government intervention is necessary. This decision must be based on sound Catholic social principles.

Background for Development:

introduction: Over the past two or three years we have seen lengthly and sharp debate over medical care of the aged. This debate reached its height in April and May of 1962, when the American Medical Association and the president of the United States engaged in mutual argument, accusation, and discussion. All kinds of terms were used, like "socialized medicine," "medicare," "federal health insurance," etc. This debate is merely one aspect of a general debate now going on among Americans on the proper role of government in modern life.

No one is unaffected by the regulations of the federal government.

Businessmen discuss and argue over the regulations put out by the Securities and Exchange Commisison. Union men are concerned with decisions of the National Labor Relations Board. TV and radio are under the control of the Federal Communications Commission. The Interstate Commerce Commission affects many phases of life. The Federal Aviation Administration controls the safety of our airlines and airports. There are hundreds of such commissions. All of us have been affected by them. Many have received their education under the G. I. bill of rights. Most of us have been given medicines by our doctors which were the result of federally financed research. The homes we live in may have been financed by the FHA. Our educational system, our family lives, our local communities with their problems of urban renewal, and all aspects of our life are greatly influenced by federal laws and regulations. Most of us do not know how to judge this federal intervention in our lives. We often are like the man in the airport who was condemning federal intervention in business but who at the same time resolved to get the FAA after an airline whose planes were consistently late. We must ask ourselves whether there is a Catholic viewpoint on the proper role of government, especially the federal government, in business, education, health, city planning, etc.

1. The first principle which we must consider is what is our basic attitude towards the government. Catholic social thinkers hold that the government is not the enemy of the people. It is supposed to be the protector of the people. But it is also clearly apparent that the state is not the whole reason for man's existence. Government is not the master of the people. Communism, nazism, fascism, and all other forms of government based on the idea that the state has total control of the population have long been condemned by the Church. To use a phrase from Maritain, the state (the government) is the highest expression of the will of the people. This one point, then, must be kept firmly in mind; the state exists for the people, and not the people for the state. In a certain sense, everyone from the president down to the lowest man on the totem pole of political power is a servant of the people.

2. The second principle is that in modern society it is necessary for the state to involve itself in many things in which, at one time, it had little or no interest. Pope Pius XI in Quadragesimo Anno said: ". . . As a result of these steady and tireless efforts, there has arisen a new branch of law, unknown to earlier times, whose aim is the energetic defense of those sacred rights of the workingman which proceed from his dignity as man and as a Christian. These laws concern the soul, the health, the strength, the family, housing, workshops, wages, dangerous

employments, in a word, all that affects the wage earners, with particular regard to women and children. . . ."

In a complex society such as ours the federal government has intervened in other things besides labor-management disputes. Our country needed better roads; therefore we have the billion dollar highway program. No city or state could undertake such a vast program. Only the federal government could. We needed a G. I. Bill of Rights after the war. We need better housing and help for the average man to own his own home; therefore, federal bureaus have had to be developed. As long as these bureaus do what small units of society cannot do, and as long as citizens maintain the right to elect the officials who run the government and their right to speak out, the increasing federal power need not be feared.

In Catholic social thought, however, two misstatements are to be avoided. Number one: "governmental intervention is always to be avoided." Number two: "governmental intervention must always be sought." The proper statement is this: where there is a true need, then governmental intervention on the federal level is necessary and should be demanded. John XXIII (Christianity and Social Progress) said: "But in this matter . . . it is necessary that public authorities take active interest, the better to increase output of goods and to further social progress for the benefit of all citizens. This intervention that encourages, stimulates, supplements, and complements, is based upon the principle of subsidiarity. . . ."

application: These two principles put the burden for determining the amount of federal intervention in daily life on the individual citizen.

No one thinks it right to consult the pope on every piece of legislation. The citizen makes a judgment about the necessity of governmental intervention without a preconceived position that it is always right or always wrong. If the legislation to meet a problem is necessary, it is the duty of the citizen to support it. If it is unnecessary, it is the duty of the citizens to solve the problem by other means. Catholics will have legitimate differences of opinions on many pieces of legislation. The Catholic, himself, however, must realize that the Church does have a social doctrine which he should know and follow. This means that he bases his judgment on a particular piece of legislation, on the Catholic doctrine—not merely on the editorials of newspapers, radio commentators or news magazines, nor even on the ideas held by a labor union or a trade association.

THE HOLY SPIRIT WITHIN THE CHURCH

aim: To point out that the same Holy Spirit whose activity was so evident in the early Church still lives and acts in the Church today.

suggested introduction: Even at the very end of His life on earth, as Jesus was about to ascend into heaven, the Apostles did not understand Christ's mission. They showed their lack of understanding by the question they asked (Acts 1:6). Jesus replied by saying that the Holy Spirit would explain it all to them.

development: 1. The Acts of the Apostles describes the intense activity of the Holy Spirit in the early Church.

2. The same Holy Spirit lives and acts in the Church today and in the members of the Church.

application: We should pray to the Holy Spirit, asking Him to guide the Church especially during these ecumenical times. We should ask Him, too, to make us more docile to His influence.

Background for Development:

introduction: Even after our Lord's Resurrection the Apostles still did not understand the real meaning of Christ's coming. They still looked upon Him as an earthly king who would restore the Kingdom of Israel. Just before Christ's Ascension into heaven they asked Him, "Lord, wllt thou at this time restore the Kingdom of Israel?" Jesus answered in words which must have been very puzzling to the Apostles, "It is not for you to know the times of dates which the Father has fixed by his own authority; but you shall receive power when the Holy Spirit comes upon you, and you shall be witnesses for me in Jerusalem and in all Judea and Samaria and even to the very ends of the earth." (Acts 1:7-8).

Jesus had spoken about this Holy Spirit before. At the Last Supper He promised that He would send the Holy Spirit as a consoler. He said that it was good for the Apostles that He leave them and go to the Father because only if He did would He send this Holy Spirit upon them. He told the Apostles that the Holy Spirit would remind them of what He had taught them, would instruct them as to what they were to say when they were hailed before judges and magistrates—in a word would guide them, would give them understanding and would inflame them with zeal to do the work of Christ. Nevertheless, it must have been a bewildered group that gathered in the upper room at Jerusalem to spend nine days in prayer as Jesus had told them to. This Holy Spirit, of whom Jesus had spoken so much, was still just a name to them. Then, suddenly and dramatically, on Pentecost Sunday everything was changed. The Holy Spirit came upon the Apostles and, all at once, they understood. This Holy Spirit, of whom Christ had spoken, was the very Person of God's love, the spirit of Jesus, who filled them with understanding, courage, love and zeal. They acted now, not on their own, but according to the terrific dynamic force which was given to them by the Holy Spirit, living and acting within them.

1. One of the most striking things about the Acts of the Apostles is the intense activity of the Holy Spirit which it describes. The Holy Spirit might be said to be the central character in this book. The Apostles and all the human characters act and speak as agents of the Holy Spirit. They are activated by Him, inspired by Him, motivated by Him. His presence and intense activity within the Church are evident on almost every page.

On Pentecost Sunday, after his great sermon to the crowd below, Peter said to the people, "Repent and be baptized every one of you in the name of Jesus Christ for the forgiveness of your sins; and you will receive the gift of the Holy Spirit" (Acts 2:38). When Peter stood before the high priests to be questioned, he was "filled with the Holy Spirit" when he spoke (Acts 4:8). When the Apostles prayed in thanksgiving for the release of Peter and John by the high priest "the place where they had assembled was shaken, and they were all filled with the Holy Spirit, and spoke the words of God with boldness" (Acts 5:3). Stephen, the first Christian martyr, was "a man full of faith and of the Holy Spirit" (Acts 6:5). The people "were not able to withstand the wisdom and the Spirit who spoke," through Stephen (Acts 6:11). When the Apostles heard that the Samaritans had received the word of God they sent Peter and John, who laid hands on them in order that they might receive the Holy Spirit (Acts 8:18). It was the Holy Spirit who directed Philip to run alongside of the chariot in which the Ethiopian sat, reading the Scriptures (Acts 8:29). The whole church is described as being "filled with the consolation of the Holy Spirit" (Acts 9:31). During Peter's discourse at the baptism of Cornelius the Holy Spirit came on all who were listening to his message. And the faithful of the circumcision who had come with Peter were amazed, "because on the Gentiles also the grace of the Holy Spirit had been poured forth" (Acts 10:44-45).

2. The same Holy Spirit whose presence and activity are described in the Acts of the Apostles lives and acts within the Church today and within the members of the Church. The activity of the Spirit in the infant Church was not a temporary thing, destined to cease once the Church had grown large and strong enough for the world to notice. The Church could never grow to the point where she no longer needed

the Holy Spirit. She would cease to be the Church, she would cease to live without Him. He is her soul, her principle of life and activity. We can exaggerate, too, the idea that the action of the Holy Spirit was much greater in the early days than it is now. There were unusual and striking manifestations for a time, it is true—e.g. the charismatic gifts, but one of the reasons why the activity of the Spirit is so evident on the pages of the Acts of the Apostles is that everyone was so sensitive to His presence, so aware of Him and of His activity. If He seems less active today is it mainly because we are less aware of His activity?

3. The Holy Spirit lives and acts in us as members of Christ's Church. Christ has given Him to us. We, too, were filled with the Holy Spirit at Baptism and Confirmation. He dwells within us, directing us, guiding us, moving us to act in a Christ-like manner, prompting us to show our love for God and for one another in action, forming and molding us in the image of Christ. The actual graces which we need in order to grow in holiness are not shot to us from heaven like arrows. They are the promptings of a Person, the Holy Spirit, who lives within us.

application: On Pentecost Sunday, as we recall with gratitude to God, the coming of the Holy Spirit into the Church, we should pray to the Holy Spirit, asking Him to continue to guide the Church, especially during these important ecumenical times.

We should ask the Holy Spirit, too, to make us each more docile to the promptings of His grace within us.

TRINITY SUNDAY

LOVE REQUIRES INVOLVEMENT

aim: To point out to the people that it is necessary for the good Catholic to become involved with people who are suffering or in need.

suggested introduction: The story of Father Pire, who became involved with the D.P.s who could not find admittance to any country.

development: 1. The Catholic has an obligation to become involved with people who are in need.

2. We should not be deterred from doing anything merely because we seem to be unable to do something big.

application: If we are sincerely trying to love our neighbor, we will be willing to give time and effort to helping them.

Background for Development:

introduction: In 1958 a Dominican priest was awarded the Nobel Peace Prize. Father Dominique Pire won that prize because he was not afraid to become involved with pepole who had problems, the hard core of refugees who could not find a country to take them in. This priest did not seek the prize. It came to him because he started in a small way to meet a problem and ended up doing something big. In 1948 when he was pastor of a small parish in Belgium, he asked an American Army officer to talk to a group of lay people in the parish. The officer spoke about the terrible plight of the refugees who were still in D.P. camps. These were people who had no hope, no place to go. They were old, sick, mentally disturbed, disabled. No country would take them in. 160,000 of these forgotten people were herded together in make-shift, crowded refugee camps. They had lost all faith in mankind and human goodness. Father Pire and his group of lay leaders did not shake their heads and say that the situation was tragic. Nor did they set up a grandiose plan for solving the world refugee problem. They merely did what they could. They got the names of 47 people in the camp and wrote them a friendly, encouraging letter. From this letter writing grew what they called "godfathering." A "godfather" would write encouraging letters and send parcels of food, clothes and other odds and ends to his "godson" in a camp. Today 18,000 volunteers from 20 countries are in this program of help for the refugees. Father Pire himself has built six villages and is building the seventh, in which these people can have a home and can find work, and can live as decent people. He has also launched a world wide movement called "World of the Heart," which is trying to promote understanding among the young people of Africa, Asia and the West. This movement is also engaged in several aid programs in Africa and Asia. All this because a priest and a few people were not afraid to become involved in a problem when they heard about it.

1. No matter how respectable the private life of a Catholic, no matter how generous his contribution to charitable causes, no matter how scrupulous his attendance at Holy Mass, these will not make him acceptable to God if at the same time he continues to violate his duties of honesty and social justice. We cannot buy our way into heaven, either with careful observation of all the rules of the Church or with money offered to the right charities. Only love will enable us to attain

heaven. And love requires becoming involved in the sufferings and difficulties of others.

People today want to avoid at all costs getting "involved." Are they asked to join a neighborhood community organization? The organization is too "controversial" for them to want to take the chance. Are they asked to play the part of a good citizen and become engaged in a political campaign? They want to stay away from politics because it might be messy if they got "involved." Are they asked to serve on a grand jury? This would take too much of their time. Is there an auto accident on the side of the road? Well, someone has already called the police—probably. Do they witness an auto accident? They didn't see a thing, because they don't want to have to testify. Are they invited to join a Catholic Action organization? They hold back for fear of making a "commitment." Are they requested to help in some parish project? Well, they will help, but they won't assume responsibility. Is there racial injustice in their city? That's a shame, but they just haven't got the time. Does the Pope talk about the duty of the rich nations to help the poor nations? "That is all very well, but the Pope doesn't have to pay taxes, and besides this foreign aid business is too complicated." In short, the motto of modern man is "avoid as much responsibility as you possibly can." Unfortunately, this is not Christianity, whatever else it might be. Our Lord told us that on judgment day we will be judged not on how many sins we did not commit but on the opportunities to practice charity that we passed up—"Depart from me, accursed ones, into everlasting fire . . . for I was hungry and you did not give me to eat; I was thirsty and you gave me no drink. . . ." We will be judged on whether we did get involved with our fellow men. We will be judged on whether we have recognized Christ in the least of our brothers, whether that brother be a man bleeding to death in a gutter, a man of different skin color in our neighborhood, a man starving in an underdeveloped country, a man asking us for help in making our neighborhood, our city, our country, our world a better place to live.

2. Too often when people hear of tragic situations they are at a loss as to what should be done. Because they cannot solve the whole problem they do nothing. Father Pire never thought he would get a prize for his work with the D.Ps. when he wrote his first letter. God opened the way gradually to bigger and more effective work. A couple in Chicago became involved in the whole penal system of the county and city just by responding to a plea from a priest for books for prisoners. They ended up by setting up an agency to find prisoners jobs, and now devote much of their time to helping those who have been in prison. No one can respond to every situation he meets, but on the other hand he must not close his mind and heart to every situation until the

right one comes along. Politics, jails, our hospitals, sick and disabled people, the poor, all need people who will write letters or lick stamps. Many Catholic institutions and hospitals need volunteer help. There is always an opening for the man in any situation who wants to do what little he can, the man who is willing to become involved.

application: Our Lord had a great deal to say about love, but He did more than talk about it. More impressive, even, than His words is His life, which was completely a life of service to others. Jesus was not afraid to become involved with people. He went all the way by actually becoming a man and living a human life among human beings. He spent His time doing good for others. His love and concern for the poor, for sinners, for all men led to His crucifixion, as He had known it would. As Christians we must take as our model of "involvement" no one less than Christ Himself. We must give our time and effort, we must give *ourselves* as He did.

SECOND SUNDAY AFTER PENTECOST

SOCIAL JUSTICE

aim: To show that social justice is a manifestation of our love for our fellow men.

suggested introduction: The meaning of the word justice.

development: 1. Social justice requires that men take part in organizations which are necessary to make society run smoothly.

2. Those who are interested in such groups must work to have the group seek the common good rather than purely selfish ends.

application: Every man who loves his neighbor should belong to some group which is trying to promote the common good.

Background for Development:

introduction: The word "justice" calls up the image of the blindfolded lady with the scales. It brings forth immediately the idea of what moralists call "commutative justice." We all think of the little boy who furtively takes a dime from his mother's purse, of the burglar who breaks into a home and rifles it, of the shoplifter, the pickpocket, the dishonest clerk, the man who pads his expense account or the one who cheats his employer by loafing on the job.

Actually, the word justice has a wider application. There are other forms of justice besides commutative justice. One such, about which the Popes have had a great deal to say in their encyclicals, is social justice. Yet, despite what is written in encyclicals, we do not hear enough about this aspect of Catholic teaching. We hear much about a day's work for a day's pay and about the evils of cheating and stealing. We hear little about the obligation we have to participate in the various groups and organizations which are necessary for our society and about the obligation of such groups to promote the common good of all men, not just of their few select members. It is this type of activity which is demanded by the virtue of social justice.

1. In modern society there are strange contradictions to be found in moral behavior. There are daily communicants who talk disparagingly of minority groups and discriminate against them. There are Christian employers who do everything possible to prevent the formation of a union, even a good union, in their plants. There are Catholic union officials who act in an arbitrary and high-handed manner with their constituencies and employers. There are in our vast metropolitan areas only small numbers of people who are interested in their community organizations.

All these various cases represent difficulties under the virtue of social justice. Pius XI in his encyclical on atheistic communism pointed out that the development of the virtue of social justice would benefit society and be the social lubricant by which society functions smoothly. Social justice can be defined as the virtue which regulates a man's participation in group action designed to make the institutions of society conform to the common good in the socio-economic sphere.

This definition means, in simple words, that all men who live in a society share the responsibility with others for the good operation of that society. In other words, all of us have to work with other people in various organizations to make the society in which we live better and more Christian.

The examples of this participation are many: 1) The best planned and best directed city in the world needs citizens who take pride in the operation of their city, who share in city government and who contribute to its seeking after the benefits which a good city should give its citizens. This means, in social justice, that a Catholic should be willing to join and work in various political groups for the improvement of city government, that a good Catholic should be actively interested in neighborhood conservation and improvement groups, that a good

Catholic should be willing to serve on various committees and organizations which try to promote the civic welfare of the city in which he lives. A similar interest in state and national politics and welfare would, of course, be in order.

2) All men make their living in the large complex web of groups and organizations which we call the economic order. Social justice requires that men be actively interested in labor unions if they work for other people, in managerial organizations if they hire others, and in their own professional groups if they are professional men. They must not be content to sit back and enjoy the benefits of other men's work. They must be active in such organizations even though such activity is difficult and seemingly unrewarding.

3) There are many social problems which affect the community and many organizations which are trying to meet these problems. These organizations might be interested in such simple problems as saving the dunes or preserving historical and cultural landmarks, or they may be interested in such far reaching problems as segregation and discrimination, juvenile delinquency, prison reform, and the reform of the constitution of the States. It is obvious that everyone can not be involved in all of these organizations, but can we say that a man who is involved in none of them has a real interest in his neighbor, that he has a sense of social justice, that he is a responsible Catholic, doing his share to make the world pleasing to Christ?

2. All these organizations affect the common good in some way. These organizations must be rational and human in their operation. It is the obligation of the members of these various organizations to direct the organization to promote the common good, not just the good of a privileged group or of the few who have power. If the government acts without concern for the common good, we have, at the best, a corrupt graft-ridden administration, and at the worst, tyranny.

In the economic field we are facing our most serious battle with communism. It is the contention of the communists that our desire for profits, for higher wages, for security is so strong that it reduces economic life to warfare, in which there are many casualties. Can we honestly say that modern American business is guided by a desire of achieving the best for the most people, in other words, by the principle that the common good is more important than the good of individual groups? We hear that "business is business." We read of bribes, illegal price fixing, refusal to help developing nations, refusal of unions to allow jobs to be dropped when changing economic situations might make them unnecessary. We hear of unions demanding higher wages or more benefits unreasonably, and of corporations raising prices without considering the impact of their actions on the common good. The man who is interested in social justice and who belongs to organizations which affect the political or economic order will do all in his power to see to it that decisions are made not only in the light of self-interest but also in the light of the common good.

application: Catholics are sometimes criticized for failing to take part in community organizations and projects. To be truly Catholic we must be interested in promoting the common good and seeing that social justice prevails. It is not enough to say our prayers and do nothing about social conditions which cause suffering to others. If we truly love our neighbor, we will seek to join others in groups which are trying to promote the common good.

THIRD SUNDAY AFTER PENTECOST

SOCIAL CHARITY

aim: To show how social charity is a necessary companion to social justice.

suggested introduction: A new world is forming around us. What values are the Catholics to bring to this new world?

development: 1. Whereas social justice is the virtue which impels a man to take part in the organizations of the society in which he lives, social charity is the attitude of mind he brings to these organizations.

2. Social charity is needed in a special way in labor-management relations and in race relations.

application: Catholics should introduce the idea of social charity into the organizations to which they belong. Strict justice alone should not be the norm in making decisions; charity must make its influence felt.

Background for Development:

introduction: As we look around us we see tremendous changes in our way of life. The farm population is shrinking. The cities are growing. Urban renewal is changing the face of our larger cities. Great numbers of people are migrating from one part of the country to another. Automation and technology are changing working conditions. Science has given us the atom bomb and is pre-paring to land a man on the moon. New problems and difficulties face us each day. In a very true sense, a new world is forming before our very eyes. The late Cardinal Suhard, bishop of Paris, saw the same conditions in his own diocese, and he asked this important question, "Who is going to dominate the world?" Who is going to give to this new civilization its values, its institutions, its very way of life?

1. There are two virtues that Catholics should contribute to the new civilization growing up in the world today. The first is social justice, which was spoken of last week. This is, in reality a sense of responsibility for the good of the community. This is the virtue which impels a man to take an active part in political, social, economic and cultural organizations and not to take the attitude, "Let Geogre do it." But added to this virtue of social justice is the virtue of social charity. Charity is concern for the other fellow and his needs. It goes beyond justice. Social charity is the attitude of mind a Catholic should bring to his work and to the organizations to which he belongs.

A few examples: Whereas it is social justice which will impel a man to join a lobor union or, if he is the owner or manager of a company, to join a managerial association, it is social charity which will determine the attitude of mind he will bring to these organizations. Too often, bargaining between labor and management seems to be a power struggle. The side which has the most power wrings the most concessions from the other side. A spirit of charity would dictate that each side consider the other side's position and needs and make a real attempt to do what it can to help the other side. Thus, management would truly try to help the workers improve their living conditions, and the workers would be sympathetic to the problems which management faces in our fiercely competitive society.

A spirit of social justice would impel a man to join a community organization, but a spirit of social charity would cause him to think in terms of how he and the organization can help new groups which are moving into the neighborhood. Instead of debating how the group can legally and morally keep people out of a neighborhood, they would be asking how they can help the ambitious, hard working, God-fearing members of the group improve their standard of living. In the face of racial tension the man who has a spirit of social charity asks what he and others can do to alleviate the situation, not how far can they go in keeping certain groups of people out of offices, factories, schools or communities without violating the law.

Social charity is the virtue which impels the man who has wealth to use that wealth where it would help people most, rather than where it would be most useful for himself. A simple example: many people have savings in banks and savings and loan associations. They are usually interested solely in the amount of interest they receive, but they could also resolve to place those savings only in such institutions as would be willing to make money available to minority groups, if financially able, so that they might buy homes and send their children through college, so that they, too, could share in all the benefits of modern society. Pope Pius XII spoke of the obligation of those who have financial resources to invest their money in such a way as to provide employment for people, not merely to earn large profits.

2. Social charity is but specific manifestation of the love we should have for all people. It obliges us to recognize the dignity of all human beings, no matter how serious their sins, how low their economic condition. It is that virtue which prompts us to help people even if they do not always deserve it. Perhaps, in justice, certain people do not deserve relief. The problem of relief and who should receive it and how much they should receive is most complicated. The Catholic, more than any other man, should be guided in his judgments on this problem not only by the dictates of justice but also by the dictates of charity and kindness, which go far beyond justice. The Little Brothers of the Poor, a new religious order of men, are dedicated to social charity, to going beyond just what is demanded or needed. They try to help old people who are alone in the world. They see not only that they have enough to eat and a roof over their head, they also try to give them a few of the things which make life pleasant. They give the old ladies flowers when they call on them. They have a seven-course feast complete with wine for the poor old people from time to time. They even have a summer home for them. All this is above and beyond what is demanded or needed in justice.

Charity is not able to supplant justice. It is the virtue which makes justice palatable. Sometimes the bitterest arguments between the citizens and the government, between labor and management, and between different racial groups cannot be resolved by appealing to the obligations of justice. An appeal must also be made to the virtue of social charity, by which true love is generated in society and justice is able to achieve its ends.

application: As Christians we must go farther than promoting social justice, important as that objective is. Everything the Christian does should be a work of love. We must be aware at all times that in dealing with people we are dealing with children of God, people who have been "bought at a great price"—redeemed by the blood of Jesus Christ. In short, we must see to it that all we do in the realm of justice is infused with the spirit of social charity. We should also try to communicate our attitude to others with whom we work in various organizations.

"I WAS HOMELESS AND YOU TOOK ME IN"

aim: To show that the elimination of bad housing is the concern of all Christians, even those who live in neighborhoods in which such conditions do not exist.

suggested introduction: Many of God's children live in homes which are really unfit for human beings.

development: As Catholics, we all should be trying to do something to eliminate bad housing in our city.

application: We can help overcome bad housing by being active in community organizations.

Background for Development:

introduction: For a four-cent postcard you can obtain from the United States Department of Agriculture, Washington, D.C., a pamphlet on how to build healthy barns for animals—what is required in light, air, and space. From reading it, you will find that the standards set for healthy animals surpass those enjoyed by thousands of human beings in our city and by millions in rural and urban America.

For example, on Chicago's south side, Sam lives with his wife and six children in two rooms in a converted residence, once a luxurious home, now a slum. He shares a bathroom with three other families. The kind of home he needs he can't afford. In his part of the housing market, the demand for housing is artificially great but the supply artificially short. This situation is created by attitudes and customs which make it impossible for colored families to move.

Like thousands of other families in worn-out neighborhoods, Sam's family is a renter, not an owner. The owners, who are absentees, are concerned not about families and their welfare, but only about a return on their investment. Per square foot, families such as Sam's pay more rent than families on Lake Shore Drive. For what they get, they pay more than families anywhere in Chicago. The same situation exists in other cities and even in rural areas. Many people in the U.S. are not adequately housed.

Many other families in run-down neighborhoods are trying to be owners. They are buying homes on contract, but are caught by real estate speculators who bought from the previous owners, fleeing new-comers, at a ridiculously low price and now charge a price which the new buyers cannot meet except by cutting up a building, taking in relatives, and spending nothing for maintenance. This is the start of deterioration and the beginning of a slum. Pope Pius XII has spoken out several times on the evils of bad housing.

Pope Pius XII, Address given on May 3, 1957: "Enough can never be said about the harm that these dwellings do the families condemned to live in them. Deprived of air and of light, living in filth and in unspeakable comminglings, adults and, above all, children become the prey of contagious diseases, which find a favorable soil in their weakened bodies. But the moral injuries are still more serious: immorality, juvenile delinquency, the loss of the taste for living and for working, and interior rebellion against a society that tolerates such abuses, ignores human beings, and allows them to stagnate in this way, transformed gradually into wrecks. Society itself must bear the consequences of this lack of foresight. Because it did not wish to prevent the evil and to provide a remedy in time, it will spend enormous sums to keep up an appearance of curbing delinquency and to pay expenses for prolonged confinement in sanatoriums and clinics. How many millions are authorized for the cure of evils that it would be easier and less expensive to prevent!"

1. Bad housing is the responsibility of all of us, no matter where we live, as believers in God, as citizens of a democracy, as members of the Mystical Body. God has blessed our country with enormous resources. Slums are not His fault, but ours. We are a society of free men, and, as such, are committed to caring for each other, punishing those who exploit any man. As Christians we are charged with giving witness to what Christ meant by a good neighbor and with helping all men attain their stature and their eternal destiny even by our sacrifice. Young people—of whatever nationality, religion, or race—who grow up in slums, who are disillusioned and embittered early in life, for whom habits of study are impossible, who turn to drugs and delinquency and are on the way to becoming adult criminals, are the helpless victims of indifference and callousness. All of us have the power to help them if only by being an active member of a sound community organization, conserving neighborhoods for the sake of everybody. We cannot bury our heads; we cannot close our eyes. God doesn't close His. Pope Pius XII, Christmas Message, 1942: "He who would have the Star of Peace shine over society . . . should strive to secure for every family a dwelling where a materially and morally healthy family may be seen in all its vigor and worth."

application: A sound community organization is one that makes it impossible for real estate speculators to play upon nationality and religious prejudice or for absentee property owners to realize unconscionable and rapid gains at the expense of the community. The maintenance of building standards in physically sound neighborhoods is a rational, human, and Christian goal which benefits all peoples, white or Negro, who want to raise their families in healthy surroundings. But the first Christian goal is a morally sound neighborhood, which offers all families, regardless of race or religion, who are willing and able to meet reasonable community standards, equal opportunity and equal welcome in an atmosphere of friendliness and esteem. If we are unable to work in these community organizations, we might work on those committees of diocesan groups which are interested in the parishes in our cities. We can meet the people who live in these areas and begin to know their problems.

As Catholics we are one Church; as citizens, we are one political society. Together we bear the financial and tax burdens of renewing our cities. It is unthinkable and ridiculous, on the pretext of economy, to reduce government expenditures for renewing and conserving neighborhoods while we spend more on armaments, liquor, and cosmetics than any country in human history. People must be housed decently. When Christ promised heaven to those who took in the homeless he was referring not only to people who offered a bed to a man who had no place to sleep but also to those who help eliminate slums and build decent homes for the poor.

FIFTH SUNDAY AFTER PENTECOST

COMMUNITY ORGANIZATIONS AND THE COMMON GOOD

aim: To show that Catholics have a duty of cooperating with local organizations to promote justice and charity, instead of leaving everything to the government.

suggested introduction: In a T.V. appearance last year a priest accused Americans of lack of patriotism because of their failure to participate in community organizations.

development: 1. The popes, while admitting the necessity for government action in many matters, have insisted that what can be done effectively on a smaller level should be done there.

2. Catholics have a special obligation to be active in local and community organizations. They must apply the Church's social teachings on this level.

      application: Each person should ask himself whether he is living up to his responsibility in this matter and consider what are the opportunities of doing so.

Background for Development:

      introduction: Last year a priest appeared on a television program. In a discussion which aroused considerable comment, he said that, by-and-large, Americans were unpatriotic. To prove his point, he pointed to the failure of Americans to participate in community organizations, labor unions, political parties, and a whole host of organizations and groups which stand between the individual and the federal government. Whether or not we agree, the point is an interesting one.

      1. It is the same problem which occurred to Pius XI in 1931, when he wrote a letter on the Reconstruction of the Social Order. He hoped that the state, the federal government, would help reestablish the intermediary organizations to their proper role in society. John XXIII in his recent letter, "Christianity and Social Progress," noted the growing strength of the federal government. He did not say it was evil or to be avoided when necessary, but he did understand that man was in danger of excessive control unless intermediary organizations existed in society between the individual and the lofty power of the federal government.

      This concern of the Popes in no way depreciates federally sponsored programs which exist when needs cut across many levels of society. It simply says that men in society should make sure that local government, lower levels of society such as business and labor, should play a just part in an organized social order or society.

      2. Some may wonder what all this means to the Catholic. Some may question why something of this nature should be spoken of in the pulpit. They may regard it as something purely political, something which is out of place in church. Actually, however, this is a matter of the moral responsibility which Christians have—the responsibility of sharing in their community. And all too often Christians have shirked their responsibility in this matter. Nowhere is the attitude, "Let George do it," more widespread. Catholics know, vaguely, that something ought to be done about seeing that labor unions are run fairly, according to principles of justice and charity. They know that it is necessary for businessmen to serve the common good, not merely their selfish interests. They know that people should live together in a community. But how rare it is that a union meeting attracts a large percentage of union members. How rare it is that a large number of businessmen come together to discuss the problems of the community in which they operate. How often do the residents of a neighborhood meet to discuss how to welcome newcomers into the community and to deal with the problems which newcomers have?

The Church is and must be interested and involved in everything which concerns man. Secularists would like to confine the Church to the church building and, even there, to have her speak only about heaven, not about the temporal order. But the Church knows her mission. Her task is to incarnate Christ in the world. She must apply the teachings of Christ to life as it is lived in the world today. But how is the Church to do this? The teaching Church fulfills faithfully its duty of enunciating principles, principles which must be applied to the concrete situations which arise, the issues of everyday life. This work of enunciating principles, the work of giving Christian teaching on social and economic matters, is precisely what the popes do in their encyclicals and what the bishops do in their statements in their pastorals. The question is—how is this teaching to get beyond the pages of encyclicals, how is it to travel from a pulpit to the union meeting, the P.T.A. meeting, the manufacturers association, the businessmen's meeting, the urban renewal meeting—to all places where it will be something more than mere theory? The answer is that the Church must bring it there, and here the Church is the Catholic layman. Pius XII, addressing a group of laymen, told them, "You are the Church." This statement is not just a nice bit of rhetoric, it is simple fact; it is a truth which follows immediately from the doctrine of the Mystical Body. The layman is the Church in the temporal order. He is the one who carries the Church's teaching into the world and applies it in the concrete. This is a real responsibility which Catholics have. As Catholics they have a real commitment not only to support a government but also to make sure that other levels of society operate for the common good. People are willing enough to give money, to elect officials, to appoint committees, without any personal commitment or concern. Yet all have a responsibility towards society and towards the community which they cannot fulfill through anyone else. Each bears the responsibility of contributing to the society around them.

Today, the responsibilities of society seem too much to many people. Men tend to withdraw from its responsibilities and leave things to be done at the top, to be done by the government. This is precisely the danger of which Pope John warns in "Christianity and Social Progress," the danger of excessive control which turns man into a machine instead of a responsible person.

Society is like a many-layered cake in which each layer plays an important part. So also in society the local and lesser levels of responsibility are to be developed to make a just social order. Here is the area in which the ordinary Catholic must do his work as a member of the Church.

application: This is a matter of charity. It concerns the welfare of our fellow-man, the love of neighbor. Each should ask himself whether he has been living up to his duties in this matter— by going to union meetings, by taking an interest in local organizations in the community, such as the P.T.A., businessmen's organizations, urban renewal groups, etc.

SIXTH SUNDAY AFTER PENTECOST

OUR FELLOW CATHOLICS IN LATIN AMERICA

aim: To explain the need for concern on the part of all American Catholics for our fellow Catholics in the Church in South America.

suggested introduction: We are told in the Acts of the Apostles and in the Epistles of St. Paul of the concern of the Church in one place for their fellow-Christians in other places, and of the help they extended to one another—Cf. e.g.—Acts 11:27-30, 1 Cor. 16:1-4, Rom. 15:26, 2 Cor. 8:1-9.

development: 1. Latin America (extending from the Rio Grande down to the southmost tip of South America) has the highest rate of population of any area in the world. Some 35% of all the Catholics in the world live in Latin America now. At the close of the century nearly half of the Catholics in the world will live there.

2. Many changes in social structures are in the process of evolution in Latin America, which have a profound significance for the Church.

application: Our first obligation is to pray for our fellow-Catholics in Latin America, both for their spiritual and material well-being.

Background for Development:

introduction: The Acts of the Apostles tell us the prophets from Jerusalem came to Antioch, predicting a great famine —"So the disciples, each according to his means, determined to send relief to the brethren dwelling in Judea. And this they did, sending it to the presbyters by the hands of Barnabas and Saul" (Acts 11:29-30).

St. Paul collected money from the churches in Galatia and in Corinth for the Christians in Jerusalem. He speaks of this collection in 1 Cor. 16:1-4.

These Catholics in apostolic times showed the love and concern that Catholics should have for their fellow-Catholics in other lands.

1. If asked what is the fastest growing continent in the world, most North Americans would answer "Asia." Asia is in the popular image the land of teeming millions, but actually Latin America has the highest rate of growth of any area in the world.

In 1900 the population of Latin America was 4.1% of the world's population; in the year 2000 it is expected to be 9.4% of the world's population.

By the end of the century, the population of the whole of Latin America will have doubled. The population of Latin America will then be equal to the population of the whole world in the early 19th century.

Today the population of Latin America is approximately equal to that of the U.S. and Canada combined. By the year 2000 the population of Latin America will be three times the size of the population of the U.S. today.

By the end of the century as many Catholics as now make up the whole Church will live in a single continent, Latin America.

2. From 1950 to 1960 eight of the ten largest cities in the U.S.A. decreased in population. Still taking care of its multitude of Catholics in the city, the Church has been able to move effectively with the thousands taking up residence in the suburbs. The Latin American Church, however, has neither the personnel nor the material means to meet its population movement.

The beauty of Rio de Janeiro and the wonders of Caracas, Venezuela do indeed exist, but all around them are the shanty-towns constructed in fields, parks, and on mountain-sides by the thousands upon thousands of rural dwellers who arrive on the fringes of these cities, poor, jobless, most frequently illiterate and more often than not hungry. If Chicago had 20% of the population of the United States it would be a city of 36 million people. Yet 3 countries in Latin America have almost 30% of the population living in one city! The job of Christian education for the Church is overwhelming. There is a shortage of priests, teachers, schools, books. Hunger, homelessness and poverty make the education of a large percentage of the youth an impossibility. No wonder there is widespread fear on the part of responsible Latin Americans for the rise of communism, loss of faith on the part of Catholics and the fall of democratic institutions. In 1960 a Bishop from Chile visiting the U.S. said that it would be foolish for us as Americans to play down the influence Cuba is having in all of Latin America, that basically everywhere south of us poor and exploited people look to the same kind of violent overthrow of governments as the only hope for bettering their own lives. The tragedy in Latin America is that the few have so much and the masses of people so little. Some landowners own tracts as large as some of our states, while hundreds of thousands are tenant farmers and some even serfs. Crops are specialized—coffee, bananas, to be sold abroad commercially—making a few people rich, while the rest are propertyless and hungry.

The International Association of Catholic Employers in a recent study says the greatest problem there is unabashed hunger, hunger in the midst of enormous resources; hunger in the midst of economic greed, draining wealth out of the country; hunger that weakens millions physically and spiritually; hunger that is paving the way for violence and communism.

application: Before Catholics in this country can do anything to help Latin America they must realize that there is a problem. They should read newspapers and magazine articles as well as books about conditions south of the Rio Grande. They must realize that communism is a real threat in Latin America, and that in their concern for their fellow Catholics they must pray that the Lord will enlighten the leaders who have to solve the pressing economic and religious problems of Latin America. They must raise their voices in support of government programs which are aimed at helping these countries get on their feet. Finally, some of us might think of joining various organizations, both governmental and religious, which send people with special skills to help the people of Latin America.

SEVENTH SUNDAY AFTER PENTECOST

THE CHURCH IN LATIN AMERICA CRIES OUT FOR HELP

aim: To point out the necessity for help to Latin America, both for money and personnel, both clergy and lay people.

suggested introduction: A bishop in Latin America explained why he was not beginning to build a seminary in his diocese, "You don't build a military academy in your city when the enemy is already within the walls."

development: 1. Latin America desperately needs priests, religious and lay people who have competence which is badly needed by the Church in those countries.

2. Generous and zealous souls, priests and lay people, in this country are responding to the appeal of the Church in Latin America.

application: We can, if we have a large enough home, take in an exchange student from South America. If our homes are too small, we could perhaps offer hospitality to foreign students on holidays. The Christian Family Movement has a service which coordinates the efforts of people trying to locate foreign students.

Background for Development:

introduction: It was recently suggested to a Latin American bishop that he build a minor seminary to train young men for the priesthood in his diocese. He wasn't very enthusiastic. He responded that "you don't build a military academy in your city when the enemy is already within the walls of the city." Though in the heat of conversation he may have exaggerated a bit, what the bishop no doubt had in mind was that this diocese might well be in the hands of the communists by the time his seminary was constructed and the twelve years required to train a priest had elapsed.

The problem for the Church and all of us U.S. Catholics with Latin America is not that the Church has done little in Latin America, but that tremendous changes have taken place almost overnight. These overnight changes cannot be dealt with by the countries and the Church alone. They must have help from the countries who have more and whose population and industrialization have taken place in a more graduated manner. These countries desperately need priests, religious and lay people as well who have competence badly needed by the Church in the place they would go.

The most important long term assistance that can be given any country is to help it develop its own leadership. Many of the future leaders of Latin American countries are now in the U.S. as students. They come to know first-hand how little of our resources goes to help poor countries unless we fear the threat of communism. While here, many students, who will return as leaders, suffer from want and lonesomeness, from discrimination, become embittered and disillusioned with democracy and Christianity. If on returning home they are soft on communism, it may be due to the fact that we are soft on Christianity—that is, we seem to them not to practice what we preach. Here the Christian Family Movement has done the Church and our country a great service by the hospitality program which they conduct for these future leaders who are thousands of miles from their families and homes.

1. The Church has few lay leaders in South America. 93% of the people of Argentina are baptized Catholics, but a Catholic Action report says that they should not be considered so "because they are ignorant of the fundamental truths of their religion; they do not practice what they believe." A parish in which 13% of the people go to Mass is considered a good parish. In some places the percentage is below 1%.

In Latin America there is an appalling shortage of priests. In the United States there is one priest for every 770 Catholics. In Latin America the ratio is one for every 6,000 people. The dioceses of Latin America are now ordaining some 1,000 priests each year; at least 10,000 a year are needed to meet minimum pastoral needs. Many factors in Latin America work against the growth of vocations; poverty, consequent family disintegration, religious ignorance, anti-clerical propaganda, a shortage of good seminaries, and lack of prestige attached to the priesthood in many parts of Latin American society, are among the chief deterrents to vocations. A vicious circle exists in which the lack of a vigorous, well-trained and adequate clergy compounds the problem of religious education of the people and the training of good lay leaders.

Illiteracy is still another problem. 60% of the people in some countries can neither read nor write. Schools are in short supply and are frequently inferior. In 1959 there were 21 million students enrolled in the primary schools of Latin America, but there were 19 million school-age children who were not enrolled, for whom no facilities existed. It is ironic that in under-developed, over-populated countries there is a man-power shortage. While there may be too many people for the food available, there are too few educated people for agricultural and industrial expansion.

The Church in South America is pictured as being rich. Actually it is not so. Even in places where the Church owns property, government regulations keep the income down so that an American Banker advised one bishop to sell his holdings and invest his money in something else. The Archdiocese of Bogota has 2,000,000 Catholics, as many as Chicago, and only has a working capital of $30,000. The Archdiocese of Santiago serves 2,250,000 Catholics and has a yearly income of $165,000. A large parish in Lima has 7,500 coming to Mass and receives only $100 on Sunday. Bishop Pinera of Chile receives $50 a month plus his board and room. Another Bishop gets but $40.

With shortages in good Christian lay leadership, clergy and educational facilities it is no wonder the Church in Latin America cries out in the face of its present crisis for help from clergy, religious, and lay people from its more affluent neighbor to the north.

2. Responding to a call from Rome in July, 1960 for lay volunteers to go to South America, the Church in the U.S. has already recruited 120 people under a program known as the Papal Volunteers for Latin

America. Requests for over 200 more volunteers have been received from Church authorities in Latin America. The bishops have asked for people to do specific types of work from teaching in a University to helping farmers develop a co-op. The people who go usually promise to stay three years.

Religious orders in the United States are sending men to South America. The Archdiocese of Boston has organized the Society of St. James to send diocesan priests there. Other dioceses are sending priests to help in Latin American parishes. Parishes and Catholic organizations are taking it upon themselves to supplement the tiny salaries of the Papal Volunteers who go to Latin America.

application: It is easy to listen with sympathy to a description of the awful conditions in Latin America and to say to oneself, "Something ought to be done about it." But such a detached kind of sympathy accomplishes nothing. The question we ask ourselevs should be, "What am I going to do about it?" It is not at all unfeasable, in many cases, to invite an exchange student into one's home. The experience is beneficial to the family as well as to the student. Even people with no extra room in their home can invite foreign students for dinner or extend some sort of hospitality to them.

EIGHTH SUNDAY AFTER PENTECOST

CHRISTIAN LOVE AND COMMUNISM

aim: To point out that our real struggle with communism is a spiritual struggle and that we must win it by love.

suggested introduction: Back in the thirties a young communist "proved" that the Catholic religion was the opiate of the masses from the New Testament and the encyclical "Quadragesimo Anno."

development: 1. Communism is the antithesis of Christianity. There are many levels on which we are fighting communism. As Christians our struggle with it is a religious one.

2. In our struggle with communism we must be sure that we return with love, that we have a positive approach and that we do not descend to the level of the communists and adopt their methods.

application: We can best fight communism by living our religion, by working with others in harmony to solve social problems, especially the race problem, and by having a broad vision of world needs.

Background for Development:

introduction: On a fine spring day back in the early thirties a young man carrying a soap-box strode to the front of a large church in Harlem. He placed the soap-box on the sidewalk, mounted it and announced to the crowd which was already gathering, "I shall now prove to you that the Catholic religion is the opiate of the masses. I shall prove it from these two books." He thereupon produced a copy of the New Testament and the encyclical of Pius XI, "On the Reconstruction of the Social Order." "I shall prove my point by strict logic," the young communist went on. "My major is: any religion which teaches beautiful things about brotherly love, the equality of all men, the rights of labor and social justice, and does nothing about them in practice is merely lulling the exploited masses with words, and is therefore the opiate of the masses. But this is exactly what the Catholic religion does. Therefore, the Catholic religion is the opiate of the masses." The speaker read quotations from the New Testament and the encyclical. Then he gave example after example of Catholics who were guilty of race prejudice, who advocated hatred and violence against their enemies, the communists, who were guilty of social injustice, who were opposed to labor organizations, and so forth. It was a frustrating experience for the two Catholics who stood there that day listening to this communist. His speech was full of fallacies and half-truths, but at the same time many of his accusations against Catholics and their attitudes were true. It was useless to try to argue that it was unfair to blame the Church for the actions and attitudes of some Catholics. This was the scandal which he had brought forth, and it blinded his listeners to everything else.

It may not be true that if all Catholics really lived up to the Gospel and the teachings of the Church there would be no communists in the world today, but certainly, if they did, communism would not be anything like the danger it is. It would not have the appeal that it has to so many. The world would be so much better that communism would not find a breeding place.

1. It has often been pointed out that communism is the antithesis of Christianity. Christianity is a religion of love, communism one of hatred. Christ says, "Not by bread alone does man live;" communism is completely materialistic, scoffing at the idea of a spiritual soul. Christianity teaches that we are here to prepare for an eternity of happiness in heaven. Communism denies that there is any future life. Both Christianity and communism want to change the world, but Christianity wants to do it by bringing men into the Kingdom of Christ, in which they will know truth and freedom, whereas communism wants to do it by force, by lies, by enslaving men, mind and body. Both are interested in the social and economic order, Christianity in order to bring about a temporal order built on justice and charity, in which men can more easily attain salvation, communism in order to force men into an inhuman, grey collectivism, which they blindly believe will one day result in a classless society in which all will be content.

Our struggle with communism today is on many levels. There is the gigantic power struggle between the two great powers, the United States and Soviet Russia. There is the struggle between communism as an economic system and the system of free enterprise which the free world espouses. There is the profound religious struggle between Christ and an atheistic "religion" which is the antithesis of Christianity. It is this third struggle which concerns Christians as Christians.

2. In the religious struggle against communism there are two basic principles to be remembered. First, we must not return hate with hate, but with love. While we hate the evil of communism itself, we must love the people who are communists. This does not mean that we must not defend ourselves against the communists. It does mean that we must love them as well as all men and try to win them by our love.

Secondly, we must not become like the communists and descend to their level by using the same tactics that they use. We must not engage in persecution of others, in suspicion, in rash judgments, in name calling, in spreading rumors and half-truths, in hatred. We must, on the other hand, set about to solve great problems like the race problem, the housing problem, unemployment and other social evils in a spirit of Christian brotherly love. We may not keep aloof from these problems of the temporal order. We must face the challenge of communism with social justice and social charity and a real desire to restore all things in Christ. In fighting for the faith we must not lose charity. In fighting for freedom we must not lose freedom by allowing fear to cause us to deny their rights to others.

application: Father John Cronin, S.S., in his pamphlet entitled, "Communism, Threat to Freedom" has this practical advice to offer. "For the average citizen who asks: what can I do to fight communism? the answer might well be: devote all your strength and energy in concert with your fellow Americans, to building national unity and moral strength. Practice your religion and make it a vital force in your community. Even in dealing with moral evils, concentrate less on denunciation and more on giving leadership and example. Be a man of integrity in your work. Make your family outstanding by the quality of parental love and discipline you show. Unite with your neighbors for a high moral standard in your community. Work for racial justice and harmony. Do your part to make this a better and stronger nation, and we shall not fear what the communists plot and scheme against us."

"Above all we must have a broader vision of world needs."

NINTH SUNDAY AFTER PENTECOST

ORGANIZED MOVEMENTS OF THE LAY APOSTOLATE

aim: To explain the organized movements of the lay apostolate which exist in the Church today and to encourage our people to become interested in them.

suggested introduction: The story of the meeting between Cardinal Cardijn and Pope Pius XI, which resulted in the birth of the J. O. C. (Young Christian Workers).

development: 1. The movements of the lay apostolate are of two principal kinds.

2. Both areas of lay apostolic work are growing rapidly in the American Catholic Church as well as in the Church throughout the world.

application: By being active in an organization of the lay apostolate we show our love for others. We should pray for the success of the lay apostolate.

Background for Development:

introduction: In the Jubilee year of 1925 a parish priest from Belgium went to Rome to see the pope. In his head he carried an idea. In his pocket he carried a letter from his bishop. He expected that the letter would gain him a private audience, in which he would be able to tell the pope about his great idea. He found instead that he was just one of a great crowd which stood about in one of the rooms of the Vatican. All he could expect was to stand on tiptoe and catch a glimpse of the Holy Father. Bitterly disappointed, the priest left the crowded room and wandered through hall after hall. He walked into one room in the middle of which stood a figure all in white. It was the pope, and he was all alone. The pope looked at the priest and asked, "What do you wish?" The priest, almost fainting with nervousness, blurted out, "Most Holy Father, I want to kill myself to save the working class people!" The pope grasped the hand of the priest, "At last someone talks to me of the working classes," he exclaimed. "They always talk of the few, of the rich, of the important people. Yet a Church made up of only the wealthy is no longer the Church of our Lord."

The pope was Pius XI. The priest was Father Cardijn, the founder of the Young Christian Workers, one of the organizations of the lay apostolate in the Church. The Young Christian Workers, which trains young men and women to be apostles to their fellows in the places where they work and play, is just one example. Within the Church today there are many organizations of the lay apostolate.

1. The Apostolate of the Church is the work of Christ in His Mystical Body. This work is a work of salvation; it includes witnessing God's truth as well as bringing a human and Christian solution to man's problems. One way in which the work of the Mystical Body is accomplished is through the organized movements of the lay apostolate in the Church today. They provide an opportunity for many to work more intensively in the apostolate of the Church.

These movements of the lay apostolate are of two principal kinds:

1. The type of program which involves the laity in directly extending the pastoral arm of the hierarchy in a parish or in a diocese.

2. The specialized types of programs which recruit, group and train lay people to carry out their precise lay responsibilities in the family, work, leisure, political, and international life, and in the neighborhood or community.

Examples of the first type, which would normally be directed by the pastor or his assistant, are the Legion of Mary, the Holy Name and Altar and Rosary Societies.

Examples of the second type, which would be lay led, though authorized by the bishop, would be the Christian Family Movement, the Young Christian Workers, and the Young Christian Students.

The first type would normally do catechetical work, parish visiting, convert work, and other activities which are usually the direct work of the local pastor or bishop.

The second type would be more concerned with the temporal order. They often use a technique called "like-to-like specialization," which means that members who are workers would have an immediate apostolate to workers, families to families, students to students, nurses to nurses, etc.

One of the interesting things about these two forms of the lay apostolate is that the role of the priest changes with each. In the first, more directly concerned with pastoral responsibility, the laity would work directly under the direction of a priest. In the second, more concerned with areas of distinctly lay responsibility, the priest would, rather, assist the laity, preparing them spiritually to carry out lay responsibilities as Christians in their own environments.

2. Both areas of lay apostolic work are growing very rapidly in the American Catholic Church as well as in the Church in various parts of the world. The Christian Family Movement, which began here in the United States in 1952, has more than 50,000 couples meeting in small groups, while the Young Christian Workers number nearly 2,000,000 members in some ninety different countries.

Both works are of enormous value to the Church and to Christ. They are a mark of splendid vitality in the Church. The numerous kinds of such groups afford many of the laity of different types of temperaments and situations real opportunities for participating in the work of the Church according to the level of formation, training, and responsibility of each layman.

application: By taking an active part in the lay apostolate we show our love for the people in our parish and for other people. By being active in the Holy Name Society, the Women's Society, the Legion of Mary, St. Vincent de Paul, C.C.D., the Christian Family Movement, the Young Christian Workers, the Young Christian Students, Cana or other Catholic groups we are helping people come closer to the Lord.

TENTH SUNDAY AFTER PENTECOST

THE COST OF RACIAL DISCRIMINATION

aim: To show that the lack of love that exists between peoples of different races has costly social and economic consequences. It is paid for not only by the Negroes but by losses and costs to all.

suggested introduction: Any discussion of the race question brings a heated response from people.

development: 1. Christ clearly told us to love one another.

2. The lack of love that exists in this country and in our city has serious social and economic consequences. It also causes serious political harm to the nation because it gives the communists ammunition against us.

application: We should talk fairly about the Negro race, and not blame the whole group for the actions of a few. We should act to help the Negro advance when the opportunity presents itself to us. On the other hand, the Negro Catholics must strive especially hard to help create in their community responsible citizenship and to help their own people advance.

Background for Development:

introduction: These days, all that is necessary to catch the attention of an audience is to announce that one is going to talk on the racial problem, on segregation and integration.

1. The race problem is, like all modern problems, a most complicated one. It is a religious problem, but it is also a social, economic, political and cultural problem. Our Lord and His official interpreters, the Pope and the bishops have made the Catholic position on race abundantly clear. No one because of his race is inferior to anyone else. All men must love and help one another. Anyone who would not hold these truths would be denying a basic truth of the Catholic faith. Catholics will, on the whole, admit these truths and say that they do love one another, but that they do not want to live with or associate with certain groups of people because they fear an increase in crime, a lowering of moral standards in the community or an economic loss because of a decrease in property values or because of other cultural or sociological reasons. However, first of all, we should realize that crime, loose morals and slums are never the result of a man's race or color. They are the result of original sin in individuals; they have social and economic causes. We cannot obliterate the effects of original sin, but we can remove those social and economic factors which intensify the bad effects of that sin. Removing social barriers and economic barriers would not automatically make all members of minority groups into saints. The absence of such barriers has not made all white people into saints. But the removal of such barriers would make it easier for people who are God-fearing, ambitious, neat and honest to live up to their ideals, to educate their children, and accept our faith.

2. Catholics know the position of Christ and the Church on this subject, but some are unmoved by statements of the position. Sometimes, however, a simple statement of the hard facts of the cost of segregation, economically, culturally and politically might lead them to change

their attitude and accept integration with better grace. These costs are outlined in Grodzin's work, *The Metropolitan Area Viewed as a Racial Problem,* and in Laurenti's study on residence and race.

There have been great social changes in our cities during the last twenty years. There has been a tremendous over-crowding of Negroes into the central parts of cities. This over-crowding has been produced partially by immigration and partly by the exclusion of Negroes from housing in the suburbs and the newer sections of cities. The result of this over-crowding is that the people who are the least able to pay have to pay higher rents for poorer housing and, if they buy a house, have to pay a substantially higher price than a white family would have to pay. High rents and high house payments mean that little money is available for maintenance and improvements. It means that more people have to be crowded into fewer rooms to meet the payments. The pepole living in this area are, often enough, unskilled workers. Because of the lack of opportunity for him to learn trades and skills and because of the decreasing demand for unskilled labor, the Negro tends to be out of work more often and to stay out of work longer than the white man, and to earn less than a white man. Wives have to go out to work to supplement the family budget, and children are left with insufficient supervision. These economic pressures, coupled with certain historical circumstances, tend to make the Negro family more unstable. There are more divorces among Negroes than among whites. Three times as many Negro children as white children grow up without the discipline and security which a father provides. The fact that these slums breed crime need not be elaborated on.

Studies show that certain slum areas use up five times as much tax money as they produce. The money for unemployment compensation, for relief for ADC, for necessary slum clearance and urban renewal, for medical care and extra police protection must come from the taxpayers, not only those living in the city, but also from those living in the surrounding area. It is sometimes said that we should cut off this public aid. Such an act would not only be heartless, it would be self-defeating, since the crime rate would only rise.

The pressure of many lower income families in the heart of the city tends to lower the standards of the city. Businesses move to outlying districts and suburbs, with the consequent loss of taxes and employment opportunities. When a city has too high a proportion of lower income people, there is a serious loss in buying power and also in productivity, if the people see no hope of advancement.

An intangible loss to the community is the loss of the talents of the gifted and highly intelligent Negro children. Schools in slum areas tend to be overcrowded. Children from those areas become discouraged. They see no value in education, therefore they drop out of school. Those students who do go on to be doctors, lawyers and teachers find that they have an extremely difficult time matching the educational opportunities open to white students. At a time when scientists are badly needed by our country, an entire segment of the population has a most difficult time going to college. The number of Negroes in Chicago has doubled in the last ten years, but the number of Negro doctors has remained the same. Little need be said of the political consequences. While we are trying to win the world to the American way of life, all the communists have to do is point to the racial injustice and discrimination to counter our claims.

application: We should strive to acquaint others with the facts in the matter of racial discrimination. This is something which concerns every person, yet many white people close their eyes to the whole thing and try to pretend that all is well. We should point out to others the high cost of this unjust and uncharitable policy and show them how it affects them as well as the obvious victims. We should also be fair and objective in our attitudes when racial matters are under discussion. Charity demands that we love and accept each person as a person, instead of lumping people together in a classification with a label such as Negro or Puerto Rican and refusing to see each person for what he is—a human being who is different from every other human being.

ELEVENTH SUNDAY AFTER PENTECOST

PAPAL TEACHING ON ECONOMIC LIFE

aim: To point out what modern popes have taught on economic life.

suggested introduction: In the complex world of economic exchange which we have today, Catholics must turn to the teachings of the popes to discover how they are to serve God in modern life.

development: 1. The popes envision an economic society based on cooperation for the common good.

2. From the inherent dignity of man's work flows his right to a living wage.

application: Catholics must be aware of papal teaching on economic life and be willing to undergo the work involved in applying this teaching.

Background for Development:

introduction: The world of economic exchange is a complex one. Stocks and bonds, piece rates and seniority, tax allowances and price regulation are terms which indicate the vast scope of our economic system. In every country, peace and prosperity, poverty or wealth, sometimes even life and death itself depend on the proper functioning of an economic system. And now, since the days of World War II, implications of economic life extend far beyond the borders of any one region or any one nation. Millions of men and women are engaged in some manner in economic life. And the part they play in the economic system affects their holiness and sanctity, their share in preparing this world for the second coming of Christ.

It is no wonder than that Catholics turn to the content of papal social thought, to those encyclicals which deal with economic life in order that they might understand better the world in which they are engulfed. In this presentation we shall try to abstract from papal writings some of the basic principles with regard to economic life. Through these principles there should be a better understanding of the relationship between our economic society and our service of God.

1. In the book of Genesis, man was given the Scriptural command to fill the earth and to subdue it, to bring it into order. In a certain sense, man does this by his labor, by his work. A stock broker offering advice, a trucker moving cargo across the highways, a street cleaner, a carpenter, a teacher, a lawyer—all by their labor and their work are bringing the world into some kind of order. Through man's cooperative work, this world is made to serve the needs of all.

Immediately, one senses the great difference between the Marxist concept of economic life and the view found in papal thought. Marx envisioned economic life as a jungle in which the exploiters and the exploited, the bourgeoisie and the proletariat were divided into two hostile warring classes. Marx saw an inevitable and fiery revolution of the proletariat against the ruling classes.

The popes envisioned an economic society which was very different from the Marxist concept. They viewed an economic society as one in which men of all levels of the economic community cooperate together to secure the common good. Leo XIII and Pius XI knew that conflicts would be unavoidable, yet they believed in the essential social nature of man which brought him to join with others in a common cause. This common cause was the use of the material world, the wealth of the world, for the good of all. This is not to say that the popes envisioned a world in which all men would receive identical salaries or identical claims to property. They do envision a society in which men by mutual cooperation can secure enough of this world's goods to live decently and humanly and to have access to the benefits of society and culture.

To bring about a just economic society, men work or labor. Work or labor here is used in its broadest sense to include any way in which man cooperates in economic activity. Some view work as a curse, something which is to be avoided at all costs. Pius XI, however, states that man is born to labor as a bird to fly. Even if the sin of Adam had not occurred, men still would have labored or worked. The fatigue, the anxiety, the danger, would not have accompanied work, but men would still have to work. The labor of man is an ennobling thing since by his work or labor he uses his mind and body, his faculties, to bring order into the created world. When man labors, he fulfills the Scriptural injunction to subdue the earth.

2. Because man is a rational being and he uses his rationality to a greater or lesser degree in labor or in work, man performs something dignified, something noble when he works. If he cleans streets, washes dishes, teaches school, heals the sick, runs a machine, his labor or work is something noble and ennobling. From this general statement or proposition, many conclusions follow. From the dignity of labor flows man's right to a living wage, a wage which should be sufficient at the very least to support him and his family in health and decency. From the dignity of labor flows man's right to cooperate with others to secure suitable conditions for labor or work. From the dignity of man's labor flows man's social contribution to society.

The previous paragraph presupposes man's contribution to the enterprise and consequently to society in justice. In this view men must work or labor according to the norms and standards agreed upon to receive just compensation. Men who are unable to work because of sickness, old age, accident, or automation also have claims upon society.

The concept of a living wage has been discussed by Leo XIII, Pius XI, and John XXIII. In simplest terms, it should be enough to support a man and his family in order that he can participate to the fullest in the social and cultural advantages of society.

But man's work is not only individual, that is, it is not only meant for his own development and the welfare of his family. It is also social. Men must cooperate with other men in an effort to help economic society achieve its goal. Even though work and private property have individual characteristics, the student on papal social thought cannot overlook the social character of work. From the nature of the social character of work, we reason to the concept of community in work. Although there are different functions performed by management and labor and owners, nevertheless, each must relate to the other.

Because of the social nature of economic life, Pius XI and John XXIII recommend a sharing of responsibility in ownership, profits and management. John XXIII in general terms states that although owners and managers have the right to manage, yet workers should exercise their influence on the economic enterprise and also have a voice in affecting not only the specific plant, but also the industry and international life as well. This cooperation and sharing flow from the process of collective bargaining.

application: Among Catholics, there is great lack of knowledge of papal views of economic life. And among Catholics who have looked at the encyclicals, there is a tendency to interpret these according to one's place in the economic enterprise. What is needed is a knowledge of the grasp of papal thought and a willingness to apply this knowledge to the modern economic enterprise. Indeed, perhaps, we have a new form of penance and spiritual growth for our time. As we have tended to ignore and avoid physical penances such as fasting, bodily affliction, and so forth of past ages, the willingness to sit at meetings, to share in organizations, to assume responsibilities which sap our strength and strain our time are necessary for our day. In a certain sense, in our time, it is sometimes easier, but perhaps not as helpful to society, to fast and abstain, to cut down on food and drink, to give up luxuries as a self righteous refuge from really coming to grips with the problems of our society.

Another area which must be studied and researched by employers and employes, is the development of personality in work. It is easy to say that the workers must find a development of personality in the work they perform, but it is another matter to determine what structures both in and outside the enterprise, can develop this personality to its greatest possible limits. However, the main concern of the encyclicals is that this problem be seriously considered. In his inagural address, President Kennedy spoke of a twilight struggle which might go on for years. Although the President was speaking of the development of freedom in society, perhaps we can apply this same thought to the development of personal freedom and responsibility in economic life as well.

OUR LADY'S ASSUMPTION

aim: To show that the Church teaches the sacredness of the human body through the Assumption of Mary.

suggested introduction: The Introit from the Mass of the feast of the Assumption.

development: As opposed to the pagan cult of the body which the world pursues, the Church teaches that the body is sacred and is destined to rise and be glorified. She shows us Mary in heaven body and soul.

application: With the picture of Mary in heaven before our eyes, we should cultivate modesty in dress, speech and behavior.

Background for Development:

introduction: The Introit of the Mass for the feast of our Lady's Assumption gives us a wonderful picture, taken from the Apocalypse: "A great sign appeared in heaven: a woman clothed with the sun, and the moon under her feet, and upon her head a crown of twelve stars" (Apoc. 12:1).

The Church sees in this picture the Blessed Virgin Mary in glory in heaven, the only human person who now lives in heaven body and soul. This great fact of Mary's complete redemption and her bodily presence in heaven is what we celebrate in the feast of her Assumption.

1. The Holy Spirit, in His wisdom, brings the fullness of Christ's teaching to the consciousness of the Church in different ways and at different times. Only gradually does the fuller implication of a divine truth come to light. God has His own reasons for letting us see His truth gradually in this way. It is He who chooses the time and manner. The doctrine of the Assumption of our Lady, although already known and believed by the Church, was not defined as an article of faith until the middle of the twentieth century. Of the many possible reasons why divine providence worked in this way, one comes to mind easily. This doctrine emphasizes the worth of the human body and its sacredness. This, surely, is a lesson which is needed in these times.

This is an age which glorifies the human body, but this very glorification is a degradation of the body. It is a pagan thing. The body is glamorized; it is pampered; it is the object of great care and solicitude. Witness the sale of cosmetics for both women and men—scented soaps, deodorizers, lotions, powders and paints of every kind and description. Food and drink and medicines and tranquilizers are in plentiful supply. The body is clothed in the height of fashion. Health clubs and body building centers abound and are doing a thriving business. There is certainly no lack of attention to the body. What is lacking is a sense of the sacredness of the body. It is treated as if it were a thing without a soul, without any spiritual significance or destiny. To treat the body this way is to degrade it. The Church, too, pays great attention to the body, but in a very different way. Nowhere is the Church's concern for the body more in evidence than at a funeral. The Church places the body in a position of honor in front of the altar. She prays over it; she sprinkles it with holy water, she incenses it; she has it carried to consecrated ground and buries it with great reverence. All these actions indicate the appreciation which the Church has for the sacredness of the human body. No philosophy, no religion except Christianity has ever attached to the body so lasting a significance and promised it so glorious a future. The Church sees the body as part of a whole, a composite, a unique being who is neither spirit nor matter but a combination of both. She does not see the soul of man as something imprisoned in man's body—against its will, as it were. She does not see it as something shameful, a rather unfortunate reminder that man is less than a pure spirit. She believes in the unity of man. Her care is not only for the soul but for the human person in its total reality. The Church opposes not only the pagan cult of the body but also the heresy which regards the body as something to be despised, something which is destined for nothing better than death and corruption. The Church reminds man on Ash Wednesday that he is dust and that he will return to dust, but she also reminds him that returning to dust is not the end. She reminds him that he will rise from the dust in the glorious resurrection on the last day and live forever as a man, body and soul in heaven.

The Church has always believed and taught that the body will rise on the last day, to be re-united with the soul in heaven. We say in the Apostles' Creed, "I believe in the resurrection of the body." But, once again, the Church re-states this age old teaching and presents it to the world clearly and graphically—through Mary. Once again, it is she who shows us God's truth by showing us what God has accomplished in her. Our Lady's Assumption is, as it were, a shortened instruction on man's last end. We know that the soul is immortal and will live forever in heaven, but our imagination bogs down at the thought of a heaven of souls, of disembodied spirits. It seems vague and unreal to us. And so the Church shows us Mary, in heaven body and soul. She shows us Mary, living in heaven with her glorified body, and in showing us how Mary exists today she shows us how we ourselves will exist someday.

application: Our Lady's Assumption brings home to us the fact that our bodies are sacred. It therefore reminds us of the importance of the virtue of chastity—that virtue which more than any other emphasizes the sacredness of the human body—and the virtue which guards and protects chastity, the virtue of modesty. The pagan world, with its shallow view of the body, puts little value on chastity and sees no purpose in modesty. The Christian prizes chastity and realizes that modesty is necessary if chastity is to be safeguarded. The thought of the sacredness of the body should prompt us to cultivate modesty both for our own sake and for the sake of others. In this world, which uses sex in advertizing and holds before our eyes a constant example of sensuality, it is often necessary to exercise control over our eyes and ears in order to avoid serious temptation, in order to keep our high ideals and preserve our sense of the sacredness of sex. Modesty is necessary, too, as a manifestation of charity towards others. One's dress, speech and behavior can be either an occasion of sin for others or a means of helping others live in a Christian manner. As Christians, aware of the glorious destiny which awaits us, with the picture of Mary before us, body and soul in heaven, we should practice Christian modesty in dress, in speech and in behavior as a manifestation of our love of God and of our neighbor.

RELIGIOUS DISCUSSIONS

aim: To urge the people to have a truly fraternal spirit towards non-Catholics and to engage them in friendly discussion.

suggested introduction: Jesus at the Last Supper told His followers to love one another. The followers of Christ are not only Catholics but also Christians who belong to other churches.

development: 1. In the United States we have achieved a remarkable and workable relationship between Catholics and non-Catholics.

2. Many Catholics are reluctant to discuss religion with others. This is a sign of lack of love. If we love others we should want to share the truth with them.

application: We should never argue about religion, but we should always be ready to discuss it with others. In these discussions we should follow six easy rules of charity.

Background for Development:

introduction: When Jesus reclined at table with His followers for His last meal with them before He died, He called them His little children and told them to love one another as He had loved them. Later in His talk He returned to this theme when He compared their union to Him to the union of the parts of the grape vines which grew near the Cenacle. He was the vine; they were the branches. Because He, the vine, loved them, they, the branches, were to love each other.

Who are the little children of Christ today? Who are the branches joined in a living union with the vine? The spontaneous answer we give is that those who belong to the true Church of Christ, the Catholics, are the children of Christ. This answer is too simple. All men who are baptized carry on their foreheads the name of Christ and have His image irremovably printed in their souls. Thus the little children that our Lord urged to love one another are not only the Catholics, who have a full and complete membership in His Mystical Body, but also our separated brethren, who have fundamental though not full membership in the Church. All men who are baptized are brothers in Christ, even though four or five hundred million of them are separated

from full visible membership in His Mystical Body. The vast majority
of these people are in good faith. Their ancestors, not they, left the
Church. They are separated from visible membership not because of
bad will but because they were born to families who had left the
Church years ago. These people, our separated brethren, must be
loved with a speical love. St. Paul told us "while we have time, let
us do good to all men, especially to those who are of the household of
the faith" (Gal. 6:10).

1. Sad to say, throughout history this love has not always been
evident between those who were transformed into Christ by the Holy
Spirit. One need but look at the history of 16th century England to
discover a Catholic queen burning Protestants at the stake and her
Protestant successor burning Catholics at the same stake. We Americans
have learned how to live together, even though we belong to more
than 250 different Christian Churches. The 1960 presidential election is
a fine example of how far we have come. The political analyists feel
that religion did play a part in the voting, but they are not able to pin
down many specific areas in which religion determined the vote.

2. In spite of discordant notes here and there, Catholics and non-
Catholics in America have a friendly harmonious relationship compared
to the relationship that exists in some countries or to that which
existed in history. In practice, often enough, this harmony is achieved
by a tacit agreement not to discuss religious differences. Refusal to discuss religion with our separated brethren is a serious defect in our love
for them. If we love someone we must want to share all the beauty, truth,
goodness and happiness of our faith with Him. If we love Christ and
His little children, we must desire that all His children possess all
His teachings. To fight or argue about religion is a breach of charity.
To discuss religion calmly and with love is a sign of brotherly love.

There are signs that Catholics, and non-Catholics are beginning
to talk to each other in charity and love. The Popes have sent observers
to several of the meetings of the World Council of Churches. Pope
John XXIII invited non-Catholic observers to come to the Vatican
Council, and they have been attending its sessions most enthusiastically.
Pope Paul VI has continued the policy of his predecessor, and has met
many non-Catholic religious leaders both in private audiences in Rome
and on his trips abroad. In the last few years many books and articles
both by Catholics and non-Catholics have appeared examining the problem of separation.

application: In their charity Catholics should
have many informal discussions with their non-Catholic friends. One
woman who has let it be known that she will discuss religion has
many friends drop in for coffee and a chat about religion. She has
found that many people want to talk about the Catholic religion, but

they find that Catholics are reluctant to talk. In such discussions with our neighbors we should try to follow the following simple rules:

1) We should have the charity to assume that the other person is in good faith and sincerely believes in what he is saying. Hence we do not talk down to him or assume a patronizing attitude. We must be willing to grant what is good and true in his position and clearly see the differences that exist between the two of us.

2) We must understand that the Holy Spirit works even in those who do not have full membership in the Church and that they do possess a part of the truth of Christ.

3) We must never become angry or personal when the other person disagrees with us or fails to see our point.

4) We must realize that conversion is the work of the Holy Spirit and that we are but instruments in His hands in telling other people about the truth of Christ. We can safely leave conversion to the Holy Spirit.

5) We must know and understand our faith, so that we can explain it correctly and intelligently.

6) We must pray for the grace to understand the other person's position and for the ability to explain our position clearly. We must also pray that he will understand our position and perhaps in time accept it.

THIRTEENTH SUNDAY AFTER PENTECOST

THE DANGER OF
RELIGIOUS INDIFFERENTISM

aim: To alert the people to the dangers of religious indifferentism and remind them why it is that Catholics may not take active part in non-Catholic religious services.

suggested introduction: The experience of a WAVE who registered inductees for the Navy. It is expected that every American be either a Protestant, a Catholic or a Jew.

development: 1. In our pluralistic society freedom of religion and religious toleration are precious things. At the same time we must be on guard against religious indifferentism.

2. Catholics must love, associate with, meet with and try better to understand those of other faiths, but never forget that there are real

and essential doctrinal differences that exist and must not be "watered down."

3. Because of a basic doctrine of the Church, Catholics may not take active part in non-Catholic religious services.

Background for Development:

introduction: A young lady who was a WAVE in the second world war and worked as a clerk, registering inductees for the Navy, reported the procedure which she had been told to follow. She was to ask each man about his religion. If he hesitated, as many did, she was to ask, "Are you Jewish?" then "Are you Catholic?" If the answer to both questions was in the negative, she was to write "Protestant" after the man's name. This is only one of the many indications of something which sociologists tell us: an American is expected to be a Protestant or a Catholic or a Jew.

1. To be a normal American one is "expected" to belong to one of the three large religious groups. Apart from that, he is expected to be "just like everyone else." On the one hand, it is a wonderful thing that Americans of different religions have managed to live together in peace and harmony, enjoying religious freedom and granting religious tolerance to one another. On the other hand, it is necessary always to be on guard against one great danger—religious indifferentism. There are many people who honestly feel that one religion is as good as another, that all religions are really the same. It is almost an accepted American idea that, while membership in one of the three great religious groups is expected, it doesn't really matter which, because, after all, it is all the same. Furthermore, religious sociologists tell us that the attitudes of people on moral issues are, by and large, determined by their social environment rather than by the teachings of their Church.

It is very important that Catholics work together with and associate with people of other faiths. It is essential that they respect those of other faiths and love them. It is very desirable that they discuss religious questions candidly and charitably, as was said last Sunday. But it is essential that they keep in mind the very real doctrinal differences which exist.

There is a danger which could be present, a tendency to underplay the differences which do exist between Catholics and others. Cardinal Bea characterizes it in this way. "Living in a world bubbling over with ideas, with different and contradictory philosophical and religious ideas, one is probably too inclined toward a certain connivance, toward a certain indifferentism, toward being ashamed of the intransigence of Catholic dogma, as though it was something narrow-minded, not very modern, not very open to reality, almost fanatic. Moreover, an ill-understood love of unity and of separated brethren sometimes pushes one toward a false "irenicism." *Position of Catholics Regarding Church Unity.* This attitude is usually not openly proposed, but it is much more prevalent than we think. Research has shown that some Catholics will answer that they believe that there is only one Church and that her doctrines are infallibly true if they are asked these points directly, but that many of them really do not accept these ideas. They have absorbed some of the religious indifferentism which prevades our culture. A recent survey, made by the Cana Conference among couples at Pre-Cana revealed a shocking contradiction between what many Catholics believe "officially" and what they really think as they honestly fill out a questionnaire.

2. What then is the Catholic attitude in dealing with Protestants and the people of the separated Eastern Churches on matters of religion? We must assume that they are men of good will. We must realize that their ancestors, not they, left the Church and that in many cases they did not willingly leave the Church. The Church was taken from them by violence or fraud. We must desire most earnestly to have union with these people, and we must make every effort to understand them. But we must always take diligent care to assure the soundness of our own faith, and we must protect the integrity of our Catholic dogma. We can never compromise what we believe. We may rephrase our traditional way of expressing the truth in order to make it more intelligible and acceptable to our separated brethren, but we may never water down the truth itself. We must study to distinguish more clearly those things which are truly dogmas of the faith and those which are but cultural manifestations of the faith of western man, but we must remain committed to the fullness of Catholic doctrine. We must make every effort to discover what we have in common with Protestants and the Orthodox, but we must also be conscious of the fact that, although we have a great common heritage, we also have sharp, real and important differences.

3. These differences of doctrine are the reason why we cannot do certain things with non-Catholics. For example, we may not take an active part in a non-Catholic service, because we firmly believe that the Catholic Church is the one and only Church of Christ and that it is through her that God is to be worshipped. Non-Catholics who attend their own services are in good faith, and surely they please God by their worship. But a Catholic who would take an active part in such services would not be pleasing God. Sponsors for baptism are taking an active part in that religious service. People who are not full members of the Church cannot be sponsors. Nor can Catholics be sponsors for non-Catholic baptisms.

Great tact is necessary in explaining the reasons why Catholics may not take active part in non-Catholic services. Catholics should point out that the basis is a doctrinal one. Non-Catholics realize that there are fundamental doctrinal differences between them and us. Usually they understand and respect us all the more for being true to our convictions.

The Church now, however, to use the words of Vatican Council II, "adopts a rather mild policy" to worship in common and actually recommends it to Catholics "as a means of salvation and an example of charity among Christians." The Council, in its decrees on Ecumenism and the Oriental Churches as promulgated on November 21, 1964, declared: "There are two main principles governing the practice of such common worship: first, the bearing witness to the unity of the Church, and secondly, the sharing in the means of grace. Witness to the unity of the Church very generally forbids common worship to Christians but the grace to be had from it sometimes commends this practice." However, when and where and with whom this participation in the sacred functions of others may take place is to be decided by the proper ecclesiastical authorities.

application: As Catholics we should be thoroughly acquainted with the teachings of our Church. All to often Catholics themselves have mistaken ideas of certain doctrines and give the wrong impression to those outside the Church. Catholics cannot hope to get sufficient knowledge of their faith from the Sunday sermon only. Therefore, they should attend meetings where they will get additional instruction, join study groups or purchase books and study the faith for themselves.

FOURTEENTH SUNDAY AFTER PENTECOST

WORK IS AN EXPRESSION OF LOVE

aim: To show that the work which a person does not only benefits himself and his family, but also contributes to the good of others; therefore it is a manifestation of love for others.

suggested introduction: Every building could well bear a plaque to the men who worked on it, because each one gave something of himself to the building.

development: 1. God "worked" when he made the world. This "work" of God was prompted by love for others. The work a man does is a manifestation of his love and concern for others.

These are (*a*)his family, (*b*) people all over the world, who supply the materials he needs or who use the products he makes, (*c*) the other people in his plant or office.

2. Men must do their work well because it is a manifestation of their desire not only to make a living but also to serve other people.

application: Men should offer their work to God in the Mass.

Background for Development:

introduction: A young man was graduated from Loyola University a few years ago with a master's degree in the social sciences. While going to school and after graduation he worked as a common laborer, helping to build the Chicago subway and many of the tall buildings that one can now see in the loop. His friends could not understand why he kept at such "menial" labor. His answer was that he wanted the joy of one day pointing out to his children what he had helped to build.

Many a man dies in the construction of buildings, bridges, etc. No monument is erected to them, but one might be. In fact, a plaque might be erected at every building bearing on it the names of those who have worked on it, because all have given of their lives. And a similar plaque might be erected at every factory, at every steelmill, at every office, with names on it—names of real people, important people each one of them, not just social security numbers. And they all give of their lives.

1. God the creator is pictured in the Old Testament as a good workman, slowly forming in His hands the earth and the cosmos, the sky, the ground we walk on, the birds, the fishes, the plants, the animals, and finally man. All this is a work of God's love. God needs nothing that He creates; He has created all things for His eternal Son and His adopted sons. He has created man in His image so that man, too, can work and labor for others out of love.

A man kisses his wife goodbye on his way to work and similarly when he returns. All that he does at work has been embraced in that love, love for his wife and children. At the same time, his work is done for other families and the whole human family. His children don't wear all the shoes he makes; and if he makes shoes, someone else makes autos, furniture, handles food, provides medical care, teaches his children. All work binds men together. It is mutual interdependence; it is service we give and depend upon. It is love.

Work is also a link to the world. As man today approaches the realization of a world community, his interdependence becomes more pronounced. The cabinet-maker in Chicago finds it hard to live without the raw material furnished by the woodsman of Canada, or the jeweler in Detroit without the gold furnished by the miner in Africa. Work provides a bond of unity, man to man, and culture to culture. As a mutual service of free men it provides a deeper understanding of the place of social love (not social almsgiving) in our present industrialized world. The engineer, the agricultural expert, the fisherman, the factory worker, can see his work as service to men in distant parts of the globe.

At the plant level, too, work is mutual service—not just on the part of the employees, but also on the part of the management. Management needs workers in the shop, but the shop workers also need management. The function of management is to preserve and promote the common good—to keep an enterprise productive and cooperative. Working together means much more than laboring at one address. It demands planning, efficient methods, cooperation between free men who respect each other. Loafing, either in the shop or front office, or hostile, high-handed attitudes in either place, can ruin a business and a livelihood for all involved.

The tragedy of the industrial revolution was that it depersonalized human beings in factories. For a long time this was callously thought to be good. Every intelligent manager today, and their number is growing, is trying to find ways to make every worker know his importance, the importance of his contribution, the importance of a job done well. It must cease to be true as Pope Pius XI lamented that "dead matter leaves factories ennobled and transformed, while working men are corrupted and degraded."

Work is also a bond of oneness between men on the same job—painters, plasterers, doctors, nurses, mechanics, lawyers. It is natural for men to give recognition to this oneness in organizations which safeguard jobs, standards of performance, and economic rights. Labor unions and professional organizations spring from a basic human impulse, as natural for man as for a bird to fly.

2. Since work is service, it is important that every job be done well. With everything that God made, reflecting upon it He could say: "It is good." Man should be able to say at the end of each day's work: "It is good." Careless work is costly; it has to be replaced, it can even endanger life. Despite its drudgery and monotony—and all work has some—a man who cannot take some measure of pride and joy in his work, no matter what it is, is not yet a man; he is not yet like God.

application: Men also work when they worship. Worship partakes of the characteristics of both leisure and work. It should be joyful, surrounded by beauty, uplifting to the human spirit.

135

It also requires effort, preparation, concentration and time. Man comes to the altar to offer himself and his work to God. He joins with Christ in offering himself. This is the most important work that a man does, but this work is shallow and meaningless unless the man has something to offer God, namely natural work through which he has shown his love for his family and for his fellow men. He cannot be united with Christ and all Christians in offering his life to God if the daily work he does does not help or even harms other people. For his worship to be perfect his daily work should be done as well as possible to help all those connected with it.

PROPAGATION OF THE FAITH MEMBERSHIP

aim: To encourage the people to join the Society for the Propagation of the Faith.

suggested introduction: The story of the dream of St. Paul in which he saw the man from Macedonia calling him to come to Europe.

development: 1. Since the time of St. Paul missionaries have been called to "pass over and help us." Today they are laboring in more countries than ever before.

2. St. Paul was helped by many lay helpers. Missionaries today need the lay people to help them.

application: Join the Society for the Propagation of the Faith (next Sunday).

Background for Development:

introduction: "Pass over into Macedonia and help us." These words were spoken by a Macedonian man who appeared in a dream to St. Paul one night in the port city of Troas in Asia Minor. Europe was calling for Christianity. For the first fifteen years after the death of Christ the Apostles had confined their preaching to Asia Minor. In Autumn of the year 49 A.D. God gave St. Paul this sign that the good news of salvation through Jesus Christ was to be preached on a new continent, Europe, to peoples who had en entirely different culture than the Jews. The journey from Asia Minor to Europe was not long. It took but two days for Paul and his three campanions to sail to Samothracia and thence to Neapolis, but spiritually and culturally the journey was long indeed. The Jews felt comparatively close to the people of Syria, Phrygia and Galatia, but the culture of Rome was different. Paul in his travels had had close contact with Greek Culture, but now he was going to Greece itself. In time he would go to the seat of the Empire, Rome itself.

1. "Pass over to us and help us" is a cry that has rung down through the ages as people in land after land sought, or at least accepted, the message of Jesus. Patrick felt compelled to preach to the Irish. Boniface went to the Germans. Xavier went to the Indians and Japanese. Today all the peoples of the world are crying, "Pass over and help us." There are more people living on earth today who need Christ than have lived on the earth in all the years since the birth of Christ. At no time in history has the Church been as active in so many different cultures as she is today. Missionaries are working with the stone-age savages of New Guinea, who gave up head hunting only a few years ago, with the tribesmen living in the bush in Africa and with those newly transplanted to the new sprawling city slums of the emerging nations. Other missionaries are in Japan, Southwest Asia, India, the South Sea Islands. Strange as it may seem, the cry "Pass over and help us" is heard in the very land in which Christ lived. Only one out of every hundred people living in Israel and Jordan are Christians. Missionaries are being called to help in lands that we picture as Christian. South America could use 50,000 priests today. France is described as a mission country by her priests and bishops. Even in the United States we have a vast mission territories. One of the largest mission territories in the country is on the south side of Chicago. Only 50,000 of the 800,000 Negroes living there are Catholic.

2. St. Paul had many helpers in his work. When he went to Greece he took three others with him. We do not know the names of most of his helpers. Only a few are mentioned in Scripture. When St. Paul and his companions landed, they immediately set out along the Roman military road which led to a military colony called Philippi. The Jews living in Philippi did not have enough scribes among their members to open a synagogue, but they did have a place to pray. Most likely it was a garden enclosed by a wall or fence. St. Paul went to this place of prayer and found a few pious Jewish women and some God-fearing pagan women at their morning devotions. While the good women listened, Paul spoke to them from his heart about Jesus. One of the

women was well dressed. She was a wealthy business woman who dealt in purple dyes, a foreigner from Thyatira in Lydia. She was called Lydia after her homeland. As soon as she heard about Jesus, she opened her heart to Him and accepted Him with her whole heart and soul. Within a day or two she was baptized. Immediately, the Acts of the Apostles tell us, she did two things. First she persuaded the members of her household that they too should be baptized. She did not clutch the faith to her bosom and refuse to share it. She immediately shared it with those closest to her. Secondly, she offered the hospitality of her home to Paul and his friends. "If you have judged me worthy to be faithful to the Lord, come into my house, she said. Her home became the gathering place of the tiny Christian community. She became one of the pillars of the Church and was a great friend of all who preached the gospel. We can be sure that this cost her money and effort. Lydia was not the only woman who helped Paul. There was Priscilla, who instructed the learned Apollo. Chloe in Corinth and Phebe in Cenchrae helped him. He called the good mother of Rufus, "his mother and mine." When writing to his friend Philemon he did not neglect to mention the man's wife, Appia, who must have entertained him in her home. Not all the men who helped Paul were bishops or priests. There was Epaphroditus, whom he called, "brother, and fellow laborer, and fellow soldier," and many others.

application: Paul needed the help of many people to preach the Gospel. Some of these people were bishops, and deacons, and priests, but many of them were just ordinary folk. They did what they could to help the cause. They contributed money. They took in the Apostle or his friends when they were in town. They instructed a few people. Today all of us cannot go to the people who are crying out, "Pass over and help us." Some people will go as lay missionaries; some people will go as missionary pirests or sisters. But everyone who goes to the missions needs someone at home to back him up. He needs money to carry on his work, money to build schools and churches, money to pay catechists and to run hospitals and orphanages, money to print and distribute books, money just to get to the missions. Each family in the United States will, on the average, give over $830 this year to buy arms for the U.S., but less than $4 to help spread Christianity. If we can afford to support a vast military machine, we can afford to show our love for those people calling for help in mission lands. We can join the Society for the Propagation of the Faith (next Sunday).

THE APOSTOLATE OF GOOD EXAMPLE

aim: To show that all Catholics must take part in the apostolate of the Church by giving good example.

suggested introduction: In Africa, Mohammedan businessmen are having an effect on the people because they act as if they really believe what they profess, whereas Christian businessmen give the impression that they are interested only in money.

development: 1. There should be no such thing as a passive adult member of the Mystical Body. Each Catholic has his part to play in the apostolate of the Church.

2. Every Catholic must take part in the apostolate of good example. Good example means living consistently, in accordance with what we believe.

application: People judge us on how well we love our neighbor. Each should ask himself, "Can others see by the charity I manifest that I am a disciple of Jesus Christ?"

Background for Development:

introduction: It is reported that in Africa, in the emerging nations, where the people are coming in contact with businessmen from other countries, the Moslems are making a better impression than the Christians. The people cannot fail to notice and admire the way a Moslem businessman pauses at certain times of the day, spreads out a little rug, kneels down, facing towards Mecca, and prays. This behavior indicates that they have an interest in spiritual things, whereas the behavior of many Christian businessmen indicates an attitude of worldliness and secularism. In the eyes of the people, they seem to be interested only in making money.

Here is an instance of how some are giving a good impression of their religion by their example, while others are not.

1. St. Paul tells us that the Church is the body of Christ. In a famous passage in his letter to the Corinthians he makes a very telling comparison between one living organism—the human body—and that living organism which is the Church. The occasion which prompted Paul to speak of this matter in his letter was the dissensions which were going on among the Christians at Corinth about the carismatic gifts which some possessed. But, in settling this matter, St. Paul speaks of something which applies to the whole question of responsibility and mutual

dependence within the Church. We each have our part to play for the good of the whole Mystical Body, he says in effect. Each must live up to his vocation and do his work for the Church according to his state of life. "And God indeed has placed some in the Church, first apostles, secondly prophets, thirdly teachers; after that miracles, then gifts of healing, services of help, power of administration, and the speaking of various tongues. Are all apostles? Are all prophets? Are all teachers? Are all workers of miracles?" (cf. 1 Cor. 12:12-31). The point is that, though the work of the various members of the Church will differ according to their position and their state of life, all have an active part to play in the apostolate of the Church. There is to be no such thing as a passive adult member of the Mystical Body of Christ.

2. Every Catholic must take part in the apostolate of the Church, first of all by good example. This term is so often used that it is frequently used vaguely. It should be spelled out what good example means. In general, it means living consistently, in accordance with what one believes. People are not being unreasonable in expecting that Catholics show by their attitude and their actions what they believe in their hearts. The Catholic who receives Communion once or twice a year does not give evidence that he really believes that Christ is present in the Eucharist. The Catholic who thinks and acts "just like everyone else" except that he abstains from meat on Friday and goes to Mass on Sunday gives the impression that the faith is not a new and glorious life but merely a matter of keeping a few external legal observances. The gloomy, rigoristic Catholic who is constantly preoccupied with sin gives the impression that the Church is a stern and demanding taskmaster and that the Christian life is a grim and joyless thing. The Catholic who is cold and exhibits indifference to others hardly gives the impression that the Christian life is a life of love. On the other hand, a Catholic who really understands the Church and lives according to what he believes cannot help but attract others to the Church. If people see that he is happy in his faith they will be more apt to see that the Church is here to make men happy. If he is warm and compassionate, people will be more inclined to see that the Church is a loving mother, who teaches her children to love. Some people outside the Church simply assume that Catholics belong to the Church in somewhat the same way that people belong to an organization, that they wear the label of Catholics, but that their religion doesn't really affect their lives. The example of a Catholic who lives his faith is the only thing which will disabuse these people of this idea. A group of men were getting together and buying a gift for the boss. They settled on an air-conditioner which they could get at a very low price because it was stolen. Five or six of the men were Catholics, but they went along because they "didn't want to be different." One, a convert,

refused to have anything to do with the deal. His example not only caused the others to change their minds but also won the admiration of the non-Catholics in the group. There are ordinary cases which arise every day which provide opportunities for Catholics to show by their actions what the faith really means to them.

application: Our Lord told His disciples that they were a city seated upon a mountain. They couldn't be hidden. They were on display before the whole world. Seeing them, people would either be attracted to the Church of Christ or repelled from it. Certainly the same situation prevails today. Catholics are on parade at all times. In the minds of many, each Catholic is the Church; the Church itself is judged by the actions of the individual Catholic. It may seem unfair for people to judge the whole Church by the individual Catholic, yet in a sense each Catholic is the Church. The individual Catholic layman is the only contact with the Church that most people outside the Church have. They do not know any priests. They do not read Catholic literature. Most converts can testify that their interest in the Church originated with contact with a Catholic layman whose example won their admiration. People are most apt to notice and to be attracted by the example of brotherly love Catholics give. They probably will not know or care about our prayers, our visits to the Blessed Sacrament, our acts of penance and mortification, but they will know whether we really love our neighbor. In judging us according to this standard, people are only doing what Christ Himself said they should do. He said, "By this will all men know that you are my disciples; if you have love for one another" (John 13:35).

CATECHETICAL SUNDAY

SPREADING THE FAITH BY WORD

aim: To interest the people to show their love for other people by telling others about the faith.

suggested introduction: The story of how St. Francis Xavier used pagan children to instruct their parents and neighbors.

development: If we love our neighbor we will want to share our faith with him in spite of the difficulties which we feel hinder us from doing so.

application: We can spread the faith by helping in C.C.D. and instruction classes, by spreading Catholic literature and by talking to our friends and neighbors.

Background for Development:

introduction: Today when we read of the large number of people baptized by the great missionary, St. Francis Xavier, we wonder how he ever found time to instruct all those people. He did not, of course, give them as complete a course of instructions as we give today, but he did teach them the fundamentals of Christianity. In a letter he wrote to a friend he outlined his plan. When he planned to go to a part of India which spoke a very different language called Tamil, he found someone to translate the sign of the cross, the Creed, the commandments, the Our Father, the Hail Mary and the Confiteor. He learned the translation by heart, because he had a difficult time learning new languages. After he had memorized the prayers in Tamil, he went through the streets of the town ringing a bell to gather as many children and adults as he could. When he gathered an audience, he spoke to them through an interpreter or as best he could, but he taught them the prayers which he had so laboriously memorized. Then he arranged for the children to go home and teach the lesson to their fathers, mothers, brothers, sisters and neighbors. Once a week he would have all these people gather and repeat the prayers aloud with him. For four months he taught the children, who taught the adults. Thus he prepared a large group for Baptism.

1. The same problem that faced St. Francis faces the Church today. There are so many people to be taught and too few priests and nuns. The lay people must help with the proclamation of the Gospel. Our Lord commanded the Apostles to preach the Gospel to every creature. He knew that they themselves would never be able to talk to each man. They would need helpers. Indeed St. Paul, who consecrated St. Timothy a bishop advised him, "The things that you have heard from us through many witnesses, commend to trustworthy men who shall be competent in turn to teach others" (2 Tim. 2:2).

The great desire of Jesus was that all men should hear and accept His Gospel. Through the grace of God we have heard and accepted the Gospel. Now we must show our love and gratitude for this privilege by telling others of the faith. Our love for God and our fellow men should impel us to proclaim to one and all the truths and mysteries of Christ.

Most people, when they are told that they have an obligation in love to tell other people about Christ, protest that they do not know enough. The little boys and girls who helped Francis Xavier knew only the halting lessons he had taught them in the square each morning.

Most people forget that all the instructions they have had and the sermons they have heard have made some impression on their memories. All they have to do is make a real effort to call forth his knowledge. Secondly, lack of knowledge can be overcome by study. When we have a strong enough motive for learning, most of us can learn rather quickly. What stronger motive could we have than a desire to show our love for God and our neighbor in a concrete way? Thirdly, we must remember that we do not need the knowledge that a priest has. The layman who is teaching others need not know all the theological distinctions and definitions. A good grasp of the fnudamentals of the faith will answer most of his needs. If he ever runs into something beyond his ability there will always be a priest to solve the difficulty for him.

application: All Catholics can help in some way to spread the faith by word. 1) If there is a CCD program in the parish, helpers and teachers will be needed. If there is no such program, people interested in teaching could help in a parish which suffers from a lack of teachers. 2) If there is an instruction class in the parish, lay people can help by teaching prayers to the people, by questioning them and by answering the individual's difficulties. The CCD is offering a program to train such lay helpers. Again if there is no program in the parish, anyone interested might help in a downtown Instruction Class Center or in a parish where trained helpers are needed. 3) One of the simple ways in which everyone can help is by being willing to talk to others about religion. Too often, we associate arguments with religious discussion. One party is trying to convince the other that his position is false. Religious discussions should be just that—discussions which are trying to find the truth. They should never end in arguments. If people ask about some point of Catholic doctrine we should explain it. However, most of the time we can talk about subjects which will not lead to arguments. Great numbers of people are religious illiterates. They know little or nothing about God, about Christ, about revelation, about the Bible. We could tell them about these things. A young woman who entered the Church not long ago conducts her own informal "coffee break" apostolate. One day she met the wife of a Protestant minister, who talked till 3 A.M. She had never before met a Catholic who, she felt, wanted to talk about religion. So far this apostolic woman has made no converts, but she is spreading the message of Christ. 4) Everyone can distribute Catholic literature to friends. If someone asks a question, we can provide a book or pamphlet for him to read. We can leave pamphlets and books around where people can read them. One woman helped in her husband's conversion, not by talking to him, but by having good Catholic literature in the house at all times.

FORGIVENESS OF INJURIES

aim: To recall the teaching and the example of Christ on the forgiveness of injuries.

suggested introduction: The parable of the unmerciful servant (Matth. 19:23-25).

development: 1. In expecting us to forgive others God is only asking us to do what He does.

2. Our Lord gives us the perfect example of how completely we are to forgive.

3. It is especially important that husbands and wives forgive one another.

application: We should resolve to remember our Lord's words and example in the ordinary events of daily life, when others hurt us. If there is anyone we have not yet forgiven, we should forgive in our hearts now, before offering Christ and ourselves in the Mass.

Background for Development:

introduction: Our Lord's parable of the unmerciful servant was prompted by a question which Peter asked, "Lord, how often shall my brother sin against me and I forgive him? Up to seven times?" Jesus, first of all, answered the question, giving a number which meant an absolutely unlimited number of times—"I do not say to thee seven times (i.e., a limited number of times), but seventy times seven." Then He told the parable of the unmerciful servant (Matt. 19:23-35).

The disproportion of the debts owed in this parable is tremendous. The king's minister is forgiven a debt which is equivalent to several million dollars. The amount he is owed by his fellow servant is equal to about one hundred dollars. It seems incredible that anyone could be so ungrateful as to refuse to forgive so small a debt after having been shown such great mercy. Yet, when one realizes the point of the parable, it is easy to see. It happens all the time. No injury which our fellow man can do to us is at all comparable to the offense offered to God by mortal sin. Yet men who have been forgiven by God turn about and refuse to forgive their neighbor who has offended them.

The words which Christ spoke at the end of the parable are very clear and direct: "And his master, being angry, handed him over to the torturers until he should pay all that was due to him. So also my heavenly Father will do to you, if you do not each forgive your brothers from your hearts."

1. The demands God makes upon us are really amazingly small. He asks us to do nothing which He has not Himself done already and done without limit. If He tells us that we must love one another. He Himself has proved overwhelmingly the infinite love He has for all of us. If the all holy and perfect God can love sinful man, He is asking little when He asks us sinners to love one another. If God tells us that we must forgive those who injure us, He has shown His infinite mercy by first forgiving us. We had no right to heaven in the first place. We had no right to be redeemed. We have no right to God's forgiveness if we turn away from Him by mortal sin. Yet God, whose mercy is above all His works, forgives us again and again, any time we ask His forgiveness. It is little enough, therefore, that God asks of us in requiring us to show mercy to one another. As Portia tells Shylock, ". . . in the course of justice none of us should see salvation. We do pray for mercy, and that same prayer doth teach us all to render the deeds of mercy" (The Merchant of Venice, Act IV).

2. As usual, Jesus does not merely teach us in words that we must forgive those who have injured us; He shows us how we are to do it by His own example. Other men died cursing those who had wronged them and were unjustly putting them to death. Jesus, as He suffered His last agony, prayed for those who had condemned Him to death on the cross, "Father forgive them, for they know not what they do" (Luke 23:24). Our Lord showed the completeness with which He forgives by the way He treated Peter. It would have been magnanimous enough of Christ merely to forgive Peter after his denial. It was hardly to be expected that He would go ahead and give him the primacy He had promised him. But Christ's forgiveness was complete. There was no punishment, not even a word of reproach. There was only the very gentle eliciting of a threefold profession of love from Peter.

Thus our Lord shows us the perfect way to forgive. This is the model. This is what we should strive for. Jesus tells us that we must forgive our brothers from our heart. The very least we must do, therefore, is to put out of our hearts any ill will, any thoughts of revenge, any hatred. Difficult as this is to do, it is merely the minimum. If we do not do this much we have no cause to expect that God will forgive the sins we commit against Him. We do not ask God merely to forgive our trespasses; we ask Him to forgive us our trespasses as we forgive those who have trespassed against us.

Yet, following the example of our Lord we are expected to go further—to forgive and forget, to try to treat the one who has injured us as if nothing had happened. This is the way God acts with any

sinner who repents. This is what He asks of us. We might not be able
to feel the same, at least not for awhile. But God asks us to act
as if we felt the same.

3. In all human relationships there is always the need to forgive
injuries. In marriage this need is greater. Husbands and wives can
easily hurt one another. They should remember that they are not only
husband and wife; they are fellow Christians. The command to forgive
those who have offended us applies to them in a special way. Even
in very serious matters this should be remembered. When the other
person is genuinely sorry, the injured one should face the situation
with the example of Christ before his eyes. In the very serious case
of infidelity the other party has a right to seek a separation. Yet here
is a matter which should be decided not hastily and angrily but in
the light of the teachings and example of our Lord.

application: It is not very often that we are
called upon to forgive a serious offense, but in daily life there are many
slight offenses which are offered. There are unkind words, slights, selfish
acts which inflict pain. It is natural to feel resentment and to want
to repay in kind. Charity requires, instead, that we put down the
feelings of resentment and forgive rather than strike back.

Some may have been bearing resentment for some time and refusing
to forgive in their hearts someone who has hurt them. We should ask
ourselves right now whether there is anyone we have not yet forgiven.
If so, we should forgive in our hearts right now, before we offer Christ
and ourselves in the Mass.

EIGHTEENTH SUNDAY AFTER PENTECOST

RESPECT FOR OTHERS

aim: To show that charity means showing to
others the attention, respect and reverence which should be shown
them as God's children.

suggested introduction: Our Lord showed His
appreciation of the feelings of others and their need to be recognized
by curing a great crowd of sick people individually (cf. Mark 1:29-34).

development: 1. Appreciation of the worth of a
man should engender reverence for him, which should show itself in
the interest we take in people.

2. We should strive to like people in order to be able to love them as we ought.

application: Few have the opportunity of doing great works of charity, but everyone has the chance to show real love for others at all times by treating them with respect and reverence.

Background for Development:

introduction: Jesus not only told the people that they were of much more worth than the grasses of the field and the birds of the air, He continually showed by His attitude and His actions that He knew that worth and that He truly loved people. Christ simply could not bear to see anyone in pain or distress. He not only cured people, He often went to a great deal of trouble to do so. There are many instances in the Gospels which illustrate this point, but one is particularly striking. It occurs in the first chapter of St. Mark's Gospel, in the section which probably, alone in the Gospels, gives us an account of a whole day in the life of Jesus. It was a Sabbath day. Christ had been teaching all day in the synagogue at Capharnaum. Leaving the synagogue, He went to the home of Peter, where He found Peter's mother-in-law sick in bed with a fever. Jesus cured her and, for once, was rewarded quickly and tangibly—the old woman got up and served Him dinner. Whether our Lord finished His dinner or not is not certain. At any rate, as soon as the sun was down, people began to come from all directions. As St. Mark says, "they brought to him all who were ill and who were possessed. And the whole town had gathered together at the door." How long it took to speak individually to each person who was afflicted and lay hands upon him is anybody's guess, but we may be sure that Jesus did not spare Himself the time and effort. A lesser man, weary as Christ was after a long, hard day, might have resorted to a mass cure. Jesus, with His understanding of human needs and His deep personal interest in each human being, healed each individually.

1. Appreciation of the worth of a man should engender a great reverence for him as a person. This is a real reverence, which shows itself in many ways. It shows itself in the interest we take in others. We notice and give our attention to things which are of value. There are people who make you feel by the way they look at you and shake your hand that they consider you to be important, at least important enough to be worthy of a moment's undivided attention. On the other hand, there are those who make you wish you were invisible. Those, for example, who shake hands with you while looking at and talking to someone else, those who walk up to someone to whom you are talking, and, ignoring you, begin a conversation with him, those who interrupt you, those who ask a question and turn away without waiting for an

answer, those who are quite plainly not listening to a word you are saying. This is rudeness, of course, but it is more than merely bad manners; it is lack of reverence for another person; it is lack of charity. Contributing money is easily recognizable as a manifestation of charity. Contributing to the self-esteem of another can be more important at times. Some people need attention more than anything else. They need to be allowed to talk, to be listened to. All counsellors are familiar with the person who comes for advice, talks and talks on and on and then—without the counselor's having opened his mouth—announces, "You have helped me very much." Reverence for another as a person requires not only that we allow others to talk, but also that we allow them to express their opinions, even when those opinions differ from ours. A truly charitable person allows another the right to have his own opinions. He even tries, as far as possible, to see the other person's point. If he disagrees, he does not make the other feel like a fool for holding the opinion he does. He tries to shield others from embarrassment and shame.

2. It is often said that we must love everyone but that we do not have to like everyone. This distinction is made in order to emphasize the fact that love is a matter of the will, not the feelings. Charity doesn't require that we have tender feelings about people. At the same time, is it not possible that the distinction has been overdone? Has it, perhaps, helped to give the impression that the love we call charity is a completely different kind of love from any other? It is different, of course, in the sense that it is supernatural, but should not that very fact make it a more perfect kind of love in every sense, even in the sense of total involvement of the person? It is true that feelings can be fickle. They may or may not correspond to the constant, undeviating commitment of the will. It is possible to feel dislike or irritation or even disgust for someone towards whom one actually has supernatural love. At the same time is the kind of person who dislikes people but "practices charity towards them" really loving his neighbor? Would not pity, compassion, sympathy, or some other genuine human feeling eventually show itself? Is it really possible to act with love without these sentiments ever being present? It is sometimes difficult to love. It is always difficult to be loved by one who is "practicing charity on you." Would the idea of what charity really is be conveyed better if it were said that we must like our neighbor, or at least try to like him, if we are really to love him? Anyone who is showing love for another human being must at least act as if he liked him. To show dislike of a person in the very act which is supposed to be a demonstration of love would be like giving with one hand and taking back with the other. It would be saying in action, "I'm loving you only because I have to in order to please God."

application: Very few have the opportunity of building hospitals for the sick as Mother Cabrini did or of caring for lepers as Father Damien did, but there is no one who cannot show love for others in a very practical way, again and again, every day. It costs no money and takes no extra time. It consists simply in treating others with kindness and letting them feel that they are of some importance, as they are in the sight of God.

PAPAL TEACHING ON INTERNATIONAL COOPERATION

aim: To point out the teachings of the popes, particularly Pius XII and John XXIII on international cooperation.

suggested introduction: Of all human dreams none is greater that that of peace and cooperation among nations. Modern popes have sought to help men make this dream a reality.

development: 1. Pius XII and John XXIII encouraged international organization. The practical application is to be found in the United Nations, despite its imperfections.

2. The popes fear a division of the world into two isolated camps. There must be cooperation even between countries with different beliefs and principles.

3. The principles of aid to developing countries is clearly set forth in John XXIII's encyclical, "Christianity and Social Progress."

application: Catholics must be aware of the international outlook of papal teaching.

Background for Development:

introduction: Throughout history, mankind has always dreamed dreams. These dreams have led to discoveries and inventions, to explorations and victories. However, no dream, perhaps, has been more elusive nor more desired than the dream of a universal and lasting peace. There have been various ways proposed by which this peace could be secured. Some tried to seek peace through war, through the imposition of an armed peace brought about by subjugation of peoples into a state of servitude. Others have sought peace in cooperative empires and treaties which were established to maintain the peace. Others have proposed Utopian and impractical schemes to secure a peace.

In our time, man once again seeks peace, and he has placed his faith in an international body called the United Nations. What are the papal ideas of peace and an international community? What are ways in which international cooperation and understanding can be sought out. What are the means which the popes have suggested for assisting a peaceful community among nations? In this presentation we will try to discuss the growth and development of the international community.

1. In a certain sense, we can say that the growth of Christianity carried with it a concern for international affairs. When the message of universal redemption, of peace, of justice, of charity was preached a foundation for peace was found. It was the work of the Church then to bring about peace, at times even using spiritual and moral persuasion to preserve peace. Many Catholic writers from the time of St. Augustine through writers like Suarez, Bellarmine, Soto, and others have discussed a reign of law.

In modern times, the popes have added their moral voice and strength to assure peace in the world through international cooperation and agreement. For example, Leo XIII supported various attempts in Europe to solve national differences through negotiations. Pius X publicly praised rulers who sought to establish some principles of cooperation in treaty form. Benedict XV throughout the first World War called for a negotiated peace, and Pius XI placed great hope in the League of Nations.

However, it was left to Pius XII and JohnXXIII, both products and prophets of their age, to see the drives toward international unity and cooperation in spite of the various power elements at work in the world since World War II.

The Pope who sensed the growth of the international community was Pius XII. In a series of addresses both during and after World War II, Pope Pius called for an effective international organization which would preserve the peace. He recommended an international police force. It was his hope that the great arms struggle would end, and through a policed agreement, disarmament would become a reality. But most of all he realized that technological progress created a mutual interdependence which could not be ignored. He kept calling for an international order of peace and justice. Even Pope Paul VI reiterated this idea when he expressed a hope for an organization of institutions to hold the peace rather than a balance of power.

But John XXIII added a definitive concept to the ideas of Pius XII. He saw that consensus was necessary to establish a true international community. And this consensus flowed from a growing sense of inter-dependence and a realization that the same sicknesses which gnawed at the heart of communist society are also at work in the West. Nevertheless, John had a tremendous optimism that an organization for world peace could be viable in our troubled times.

So far then, the approach to international peace has been theoretical. The practical application of the principles is to be found in the United Nations, which is far from perfect. Among Catholic circles, there has been at times strong opposition to the participation of the United States in the United Nations. Yet, Pius XII, John XXIII, and Paul VI have indicated their support of the UN. None of them has stated that the UN is perfect, but if there were no such place to take the problems and disputes of nations to, we would all be much worse off.

2. Pius XII, John XXIII, and now Paul VI, fear a division of the world into two isolated camps with other nations being forced to add their support and strength to one side or the other in the twilight struggle now occurring. The Popes have recognized the basic materialism and secularism, in its true meaning, which gnaws away at the heart of western society. They also realize the philosophical content of the system which hinders growth and development in what we might term eastern society. Their hopes are based on the growing awareness of international interdependence, the desires to maintain a peace, and perhaps also the basic tendency of man himself to seek out the good society. Out of this context, all kinds of ideas and possibilities may be interchanged. In these presentations we are seeking some general guidelines and principles rather than specific ways in which the inevitable drive toward unity might be fostered, provided that the unity leads toward the recognition of human rights.

There can be no question of compromise with communism as a system of thought and belief, yet it is indicated that communism in its effects and its method of operation changes, and the policy of the Christian world toward the end of communism and the expansion of personal freedom of the world might also change. Again, to repeat, Christianity and the atheistic communism described in the encyclical of Pius XI entitled *Divini Redemptoris* are clearly opposed. However, in practice, the best method of dealing with the system is left open to the conditions of the time. For example, the communist world does not present a monolithic bloc in which each party in each country operates in the same way. The communism of China, of Cuba, of Poland, of the Soviet Union, and of Yugoslavia are not identical. That is to say, communism, because of the very forces of history, is subjected to all kinds of pressure. There is a very clear difference between the ideas of Stalin and the ideas of Krushchev as expressed in the 1961 Draft Program of the Communist Party of the Soviet Union. In the political field, it takes great skill and ingenuity to realize the basic sameness of communism in principle and yet to deal with its different expressions in our time.

3. John XXIII in "Christianity and Social Progress," states that perhaps the greatest problem of our time is the relationship between the developed and the developing nations of the world. With characteristic kindness, John never uses the term underdeveloped since he realizes that many nations economically poor have cultures which are respected and ancient. He endorses the principle of foreign aid, aid between private and public sectors of the international economy. This statement does not prevent criticism of foreign aid programs, but the principle of foreign aid is clear and evident in "Christianity and Social Progress." We can debate the nature and kind of aid or trade with the various nations of the world, but the principle of foreign aid both by the public and private sector of the economy is clearly established. For a time, aid to developing nations of the world was denounced in some Catholic circles; but in view of the teaching of Pius XII and John XXIII, such a position of principle is untenable for Catholics.

Another aspect of relationships with other nations in the world is the consideration of their political and social systems. John XXIII, in a word of warning to both communist and non-communist society, cautions nations to respect the cultures and systems of developing nations. In his mind, he warned against a new colonialism which might simply replace the older forms known in the past. It is not always easy to separate aid for development and aid for political support, yet John hopes that aid from a developed nation would be given from a disinterested viewpoint. But implied in the mind of John XXIII is an appreciation of cultures different from that of the giving nation, as well as a realization that economic systems may develop according to the free choice of peoples in a country.

application: The student of papal social thought as well as the Catholic layman with an influence in society should be aware of the international outlook of the papal documents. Popes in history have insisted upon the development of international law. They have also insisted that morality has a place in the relationships among nations just as it has among men. Peace and unity but not necessarily uniformity are the aims of international life coupled with a recognition of basic human rights in all countries. The securing of peace and unity, of protecting the rights of all citizens are not easy tasks. But as men become aware of the implications of international relationships we can draw ever closer to the establishment of a true world community.

THE CHURCH IS OUR UNION IN GOD

aim: To show that we should have a special love for the members of the Church.

suggested introduction: The early Christian community at Jerusalem, described in the Acts of the Apostles (4:32-35), showed the unity which exists among the members of the Church.

development: 1. Objectively, the union which exists among the members of the Church is the closest of all unions. It is the living, organic union of all in the Mystical Body of Christ.

2. The parish should provide a manifestation of the union and love which objectively exists among the members of the Church.

application: Catholics should know fellow parishioners and take part in parish life.

Background for Development:

introduction: "Now the multitudes of the believers were of one heart and one soul, and not one of them said that anything he possessed was his own, but they had all things in common. And with great power the apostles gave testimony to the resurrection of the Lord; and great grace was in them all. Nor was there anyone among them in want. For those who owned lands or houses, would sell them and bring the price of what they sold and lay it at the feet of the apostles, and distribution was made to each, according as any one had need" (Acts 4:32-35).

Thus the Acts of the Apostles describes the intense spirit of community which marked the Church in its early infancy. The earliest Catholics were not merely a group which believed the same truths and accepted the same authority. They were a close brotherhood. There was great fellowship among them. Everyone knew everyone else. Everyone was important as a member of the community. If one member was sick and unable to be with the others at Communion, a deacon brought Communion to him, so that he might be united to the others in the Lord's body even though separated geographically. Mass was preceded by a common meal, which was called the "Love Feast." Deacons saw to it, in the name of the whole Christian community, that widows and the poor were provided for.

1. It was not to be expected that the intense community life of the early Church would continue for long. As soon as the Church really began to grow, such a common life became impossible. But it is important to realize that the brotherhood and union of which this early community at Jerusalem was merely a manifestation, is something essential in the Church, something which must always be there, no matter how the Church increases in numbers, no matter how widely she spreads herself throughout the world.

Theologically, the union of the members of the Church is most solidly established. It is a union which is closer than the union of members within a family. It is a living organic union which can best be compared to the union of the various parts of the human body with one another. The same one Christ is the Head, coordinating and uniting all the people in the Church into one body, which is His Mystical Body. The same one Holy Spirit lives in each of the members of that body making them one with Christ and one with one another. There is no tie of nationality, of friendship, of blood which is as close, objectively, as the tie which binds together the members of Christ's Church.

2. This union among the members of the parish which is achieved by baptism into the faith is also a union of love. Christ loves each and every member of His body in a special way, and He expects the members of the body to love each other in a special way. Catholics, because they are one with Christ, must love all men, but they have a special obligation to love the members of the household of the faith. In practice this means they have a special obligation to be concerned with the needs of their fellow Catholics in this parish and in this diocese. This love for fellow parishioners can best be expressed by an effort to create a spirit of community in the parish and the diocese. A spirit of community means that people feel that they belong to a certain group, that they are accepted and welcomed by the group, that they contribute something to the group and that the group contributes something to their lives. Sociologists tell us that the growth of the big city has destroyed in great part this sense of community. People do not identify with a group. This lack of identification applies to the parish. Sound studies show that no more than ten or fifteen per cent of the parishioners of a parish are really identified with it. The rest look upon it as a sort of spiritual service station.

The parish is a center to which the Catholics in the neighborhood come to worship, to learn, to receive God's help and grace, to ask advice. They come for recreation to the parish playground or gym. They come to the rectory for help with their problems. Catholics recognize their parish as the Church in their neighborhood. They know that it is there to serve them and to fulfill their needs. What is lacking in city parishes is the sense of community. The Church is seen as something which serves the needs of all. It is not seen as the family of God, living together and praying together and working together in the neighborhood.

application: The first step that should be taken in any parish to establish this sense of community is to establish communication between the people. People should talk to one another, even if it is only a friendly greeting to their fellow Catholic coming to Mass. A Catholic should not need a formal invitation in order to greet fellow members of the Mystical Body. People of the parish should help one another when there is unemployment, sickness, death or trouble in a family. The second step is that each person in the parish do his fair share to help support the parish and to help make a success of parish projects. The third step is that every Catholic cooperate with the other members of the parish to build a sound parochial life. He should cooperate with the efforts of the priests to introduce dialogue or sung Masses and not insist upon praying alone. He should cooperate in apostolic works. He should take the initiative in joining parish organizations. He should not wait to be asked, but should come forward and volunteer to join and help. The good Catholic should be willing to attend programs aimed at developing a Christian mentality; e.g. Home School Meetings, Cana Days, lectures given to the various societies, study groups etc.

TWENTY - FIRST SUNDAY AFTER PENTECOST

THE CHURCH UNITES US IN THE WORSHIP OF GOD

aim: To show that the unity of all within the Church is best expressed in the great family act, the Mass.

suggested introduction: A non-Catholic once tried to explain why Catholics go to church in such numbers on Sunday. Catholics know why they go—to take part in the Mass.

development: 1. The oneness of Catholics within the Church is expressed most of all in the great family act of worship, the Mass. Active participation is necessary to express this oneness properly.

2. Not only the Mass, but also the rest of the liturgy expresses our oneness within the Church.

application: We should strive for a deeper realization of our family relationship within the Church and express it and aid one another in expressing it by our active participation in the Mass.

Background for Development:

introduction: A non-Catholic who lived across the street from a Catholic church once commented on the crowds of people who filled and re-filled the church every Sunday morning. "The only conclusion I can come to," he remarked, "is that Catholic priests must be wonderful preachers."

The remark amused the Catholic neighbor to whom it was addressed. He knew, as all Catholics know, that it is not a sermon which brings Catholics together on Sunday; it is the Mass. Whether or not they come because they are obliged to, Catholics know that they come to Mass, because here is something of the greatest importance taking place, even though many do not understand the Mass as well as might be desired.

1. What few Catholics realize is that the Mass is the basis of the Christian community. Last week we saw that Christ joins us together with Himself and expects us to love one another and live together in a community. Each Sunday morning Christ leads His followers who belong to the Christian community in the most important thing a man can possibly do—the worship of the Father. This worship is not only the worship of the individual, it is also the worship of the whole community. The man who takes an active aprt in that worship shows by his actions that he is interested in the whole community, that he wants to promote the good of the community. The man who refuses to act with the rest of the community in its primary work of praising God shows by his actions that he is not as interested as he should be in his fellow members of the Mystical Body.

All Catholics know or sense that the Mass is a matter of great importance. They know that it is the great act of worship. What many fail to realize is the fact that the Mass is a family act, something in which everyone in the Church takes part as one. That people fail to see this fact is shown by their attitude at Mass. Some resist the efforts which the parish makes to get them to take active part in the Mass together with the whole congregation. They remain silent while the congregation recites the prayers together. They do not join in the singing. They do not even answer the responses of the priest with the rest of the people. The reason for this "hold-out" is to be found in an honest misunderstanding of the nature of the Mass. These people regard active participation as an extra, added something, a sort of frill, a fad, even, which a certain group within the Church like and are endeavoring to make more popular. Many Catholics are used to praying by themselves at Mass, silently. They prefer it this way. They really think that this is the best way for them. But this attitude, well-meaning as it is, is actually foreign to the spirit and the meaning of the Mass. There is plenty of room within the Church for private prayers and private devotions. The Church warmly approves of them, in fact, insists on them as essential to anyone's spiritual life. But the Mass is a family affair, and one cannot take part in it as one should unless this fact is well realized and acted upon. We cannot give to God the full worship which we are supposed to give in the Mass unless we take full part as a member of the family, joining with the other members in worshipping our common Father together.

The very words of the Mass express its familiar nature. It is not the priest alone who offers this act of worship; it is not even the physical Christ alone; it is the "plebs sancta," the family of God, the whole Mystical Body, acting under the leadership of Christ, the Head. The people need to be reminded that the "we" which is found in all the prayers of the Mass, with the exception of the few which are private to the priest, is not an editorial "we" which the priest employs but a genuine plural which includes Christ, the priest and all the people. When the priest prays in the name of the people, as he does in the Collect and Post-communion, he expects all to respond by saying "Amen."

The oneness of the Church, the people of God, finds great difficulty in expressing itself outside of the church building because of the conditions of modern urban living. Within the church, at Mass, even with a very large congregation it can be expressed and felt when a real community of worship is established. This happens when all take an active part in it. Now that the Mass, or almost all of it, is celebrated in the vernacular, the people should find no difficulty in participating more intimately.

2. Not only the Mass, but the rest of the liturgy expresses our oneness within the Church. Baptism, when it is administered in the presence of the whole congregation, as in the Easter Vigil Service, shows our family unity. The solemn public renewal of baptismal promises which follows gives dramatic expression to that same unity in Christ. The Church emphasizes our dependence on one another within God's family by requiring that one member of the family accept responsibility for another by being a sponsor at Baptism and Confirmation. Usually it is not averted to, but even going to confession, an act which has the appearance of being very private and individual, is actually a social matter, a family matter. We go through the family when we receive the sacrament of Penance. We seek the pardon of our sins through an official member of the family, the priest. Where there has been mortal sin, the Church requires that the sinful member go through the family

in obtaining God's forgiveness before he may rejoin the rest of the family at the table of the Lord in the Eucharist. Finally, the Church feeds us the Eucharist as the food which binds the members of the Church ever more closely in love.

application: As Catholics we cannot be individualistic in our life of worship. We can and must pray privately and perform other private spiritual exercises. But even when we pray privately we must not lose sight of the fact that we are one with Christ and with one another in the Mystical Body of Christ. Our private prayer should stem from and lead back to our liturgical prayer, in which we worship as a member of Christ, together with Christ and all His members. We should let our realization of our oneness with each other within the Church express itself in our active, communal participation in the Mass.

FEAST OF CHRIST THE KING

THE KINGDOM OF CHRIST

aim: To remind the people that we are members of Christ's kingdom, the Church, and that we must be zealous for the spread of the kingdom.

suggested introduction: As Christ hung on the cross, a figure of humiliation and shame, there was, nonetheless, a title above the cross which proclaimed Him King of the Jews.

development: 1. The Jews had awaited the coming of a messianic king.

2. Jesus is the messianic king, although His kingdom is different from that which the people expected.

application: As members of Christ's kingdom we must aid in spreading it by our example, our word and our prayer.

Background for Development:

introduction: As Christ hung dying on the cross, to all appearances a figure of humiliation and shame, there was one strange and seemingly contradictory note. There above the man who was being executed as a criminal was a sign proclaiming Him King of the Jews. The Roman governor had written the sign and had stubbornly refused to soften it from "King of the Jews" to "He said He was the King of the Jews." Pilate did not realize it, but he was proclaiming a great truth: Jesus Christ is king not only of the Jews but of all mankind, of all creation.

1. The thoughts of every devout and patriotic Jew in Old Testament times turned in two directions. They turned to the past, back to the golden days of the kingdom, back to the great King David, back to the time when Israel was free and strong and prosperous and abundantly blessed by God. They turned too, to the future, looking to the coming of the Promised One, the Son of David, the great messianic king who would establish a kingdom far greater even than that of David.

The prophets had spoken of the messianic kingdom in allegorical terms, in terms of material wealth, prosperity, abundance, magnificence. Popular ideas about the coming king and his kingdom varied considerably. Some, remembering the words of the Book of Daniel, thought of a sort of superman who would come on the clouds of heaven and in an instant establish his kingdom. The idea of a military leader was popular, one who would free the Jews from Roman domination and restore the Kingdom of Israel, giving the people of God the freedom they deserved and longed for. The kingdom was thought of as a perfect world, in which all the nations of the earth would look to Jerusalem as the center, in which the descendants of Abraham would be the chief members. The kingdom would endure, some thought, for a thousand years, others thought forever.

2. After four hundred years of silence from heaven, after four hundred years without a prophet, finally there came a man sent by God. John the Baptist preached in the desert. His message was a most exciting one—the messianic king was already here, among the people. He had not yet proclaimed himself, but he soon would. Now it was time to prepare one's heart in order to be ready to join the Kingdom. Shortly thereafter John pointed to a young carpenter walking along the banks of the Jordan and announced that this was the long expected king. He wore no crown. He was not dressed in royal robes. He had no army. Still the two young men to whom John the Baptist pointed Him out accepted Him. So did the others whom He called to be His apostles. So did some of the people who heard Him speak and saw the wonders He performed. But the people turned from Him when He refused the earthly crown they offered Him. If He was not to be the kind of king they expected they would have none of Him. Even the Apostles persisted in believing that, after all, He would turn out to be the military leader they hoped for, who would restore the kingdom of Israel.

Jesus continued to speak of His kingdom. He used parable after parable to describe it. It would be a kingdom which would begin as a very small thing, like a mustard seed, and slowly grow into something very large and world-wide. It would not have the worldly power and glory which the Jews expected. It would contain both good and bad until the end of the world, like the wheat field which was oversown with cockle or the net which held both good and bad fish. It would be for all men; no one people would have the first places in it. It would grow and extend itself throughout the whole world until the end of time. Then Christ would come again, this time on the clouds of heaven, the victorious, triumphant king, who would gather all His loyal subjects and inaugurate His perfect and everlasting kingdom in heaven. Only on Pentecost did the apostles finally understand what this kingdom of Christ was—the Church on earth, growing and applying Christ's redemption to men until the end of the world, when it would issue into the everlasting heavenly kingdom of Christ.

We, today, are the members of Christ's kingdom. We are the spiritual children of Abraham, the inheritors of the great promise God made to him. We enjoy not the material riches which the Jews of old associated with the kingdom of the Messiah, but incomparably greater spiritual riches. We are subjects of Christ the king, Christ who has given us a share in the life of God, who teaches us and gently guides us to our everlasting home in His eternal kingdom—that kingdom which is described so beautifully in the Preface of the Mass of the feast of Christ the King: ". . . a universal and everlasting kingdom, a kingdom of truth and life, of holiness and grace, a kingdom of justice, of love and of peace."

application: Christ's kingdom is here, and yet it is still to come. In the Lord's Prayer we ask that it might come. It is here in the Church militant. It comes here on earth the more it grows and leavens the world. It will come finally and completely when all who accept Christ's salvation will have joined His kingdom, and Christ will present to His Father a perfect kingdom "the Church in all her glory, not having spot or wrinkle or any such thing but . . . holy and without blemish" (Ephes. 5:27).

As members of Christ's kingdom we must all do our part to spread the kingdom. By our example we must show others what it means to belong to Christ's kingdom. By our words we must speak to others about the Church and invite them to learn about Christ's kingdom. By our prayers we must ask God to bring all men who love and accept Jesus Christ into full membership in His kingdom, the Church on earth, so that within that kingdom we may all be one, as Christ the King prayed that we would be.

THE BEATITUDES

aim: To show that living the Beatitudes brings the only true success—the possession of eternal life—as it did for the saints we honor on the Feast of All Saints.

suggested introduction: The scene on the Mount of the Beatitudes, described by St. Matthew (5:1-12).

development: 1. It requires great faith and confidence in Christ to accept the Beatitudes, since the world and our own feelings give us different standards.

2. The Feast of All Saints is a vindication of the truth of Christ's words in the Beatitudes.

application: We should examine our conscience not just according to the Ten Commandments, but according to the Beatitudes. Our aim should be not merely to be free from sin but to live according to these standards of the Chritsian life.

Background for Development:

introduction: The Gospel of the Mass for the Feast of All Saints presents one of the most familiar and most appealing pictures in the Gospels. St. Matthew pictures Jesus sitting on a hill, teaching the crowds gathered below, expressing the very heart and spirit of the Christian life in the comparable words of the Sermon on the Mount. This whole sermon is epitomized in the Beatitudes, with which the sermon opens (Cf. Matth. 5:1-12).

1. It requires great faith, great confidence in Christ, to accept the Beatitudes. They run counter to everything the world tells us about achieving happiness. The world tells us to make money, to surround ourselves with all the luxuries which the amazing productivity of our industry can provide, all the gadgets, the labor saving devices, the things which supply pleasure, the status symbols, all the material things which modern man values so much. The world gives us the impression that it is the possession of wealth and of these material things which will bring us happiness and that the lack of them will make us unhappy. There is an ever-increasing desire for more and more, as our standard of living rises even higher. The best brains in the advertising industry are busy creating new needs and promising that it is the fulfillment of these needs which will bring us happiness. Jesus says just the opposite. He tells us that in order to be happy we must be poor in spirit, that

we must not thirst for material things, must not give our hearts to them or depend on them for our happiness. We will be happy, our Lord says, if we use these things only insofar as they lead us to God, being ready to give them up whenever they interfere with our service of God or compete with our love of Him.

The world tells us to assert ourselves, to push ourselves ahead of others, to get to the top, even though the climb may necessitate selfishness and ruthlessness. It tells us to fight back and get even with those who injure us. Our Lord tells us that to be happy we must have something which the world despises and ridicules—meekness. He says that we must forgive those who injure us and must love our enemies.

Our very nature shrinks from suffering, from persecution and from being victims of injustice. Yet Christ says, "Blessed are they who mourn" and "Blessed are they who suffer persecution for justice sake."

On the one hand, we have the maxims of the world, the attitude and the example of people, and our own feelings and desires. On the other, we have the word of Christ.

2. A great vindication of the truth of Christ's words is in the very feast we celebrate today. The untold number of saints who enjoy the happiness of heaven is proof that Our Lord—not the world, not our own feelings—is right about the way to attain happiness. Today we celebrate the feast of all the blessed, all the saints. Actually we know the names of only a small percentage of the saints. We know only those whose lives have been brought to our attention because of some special reason on God's part. But this we do know about the vast army of saints in heaven—they are the blessed about whom Jesus spoke in the Beatitudes. They have achieved happiness beyond description because they had the faith to take Christ at His word and the love and generosity to imitate Him. They listened to Christ rather than to the world. They lived the Beatitudes. As a result, they have achieved success, the only true success.

The world has its own standard of success. The successful man is the one who amasses a fortune, who wields power, who is in the public eye, who achieves fame. This standard is always being set before our eyes, despite the fact that the news reports every day contradict it. How many successful business men end up tasting the bitterness and emptiness of what the world calls success? How many face disappointment and even tragedy in their family life? How many glamorous Hollywood actresses, whose lives are supposedly filled with everything the heart could desire, are suicides or attempted suicides?

Our Lord gives us the secret in the Beatitudes. They will lead us to the perfect happiness of heaven. They will give us happiness even in this world, not perfect happiness, of course, but as much as is possible in this life. They will give us peace of mind, that peace which the world cannot give. If we live according to these directions of Christ, we will have the joy of knowing at all times that we are doing God's will. Therefore, no suffering or trial will be able to disturb our inner joy. And the virtue of hope will sustain us at all times, that virtue which raises our eyes and our hearts above and beyond this life and fixes them on our destiny, eternal union with God in heaven.

The Feast of All Saints occurs at the bleakest time of the year. These are the grey days of November; the trees are bare, the skies are leaden; winter is on the way. It is a time of year which naturally reminds us of death. The Church gives us great encouragement at this time, on the Feast of All Saints. In calling us together to honor all the saints, she reminds us that we are all called to be saints. The saints we honor today lived lives very much like our own. Their accomplishments were not such as to come to the attention of the world. They were never well known enough to be canonized. They are simply the true children of the Church, who in their daily lives cooperated with the graces which God offered them, who met Christ in the Sacraments with faith and love and tried to imitate Him. We may feel that we cannot imitate the complete poverty of St. Francis of Assisi, but we can be poor in spirit, as those countless unknown saints were whom we honor today. We may feel that we cannot perform heroic works of mercy as did St. Peter Claver and St. Camillus, but we can show mercy to others as did the saints we honor today.

application: It is unworthy of a Catholic to be satisfied with merely keeping out of sin. Our spiritual life should be an intensely positive thing. Our norm of conduct should not be, "How much do I have to do? What must I avoid in order not to sin?" Our norm, as followers of Christ, should be, "How can I imitate Christ in this instance? How can I try to love here and now as Christ loves?" The Beatitudes, not the Ten Commandments, should be the norm for the true Christian.

THE DUTY OF VOTING

aim: To point out that we have a moral obligation to exercise our right to vote and to do so intelligently.

suggested introduction: The words which Pope John XXIII spoke to a group of German pilgrims in 1961.

development: 1. The Church is deeply interested in the subject of voting.

2. The popes have given solid reasons why citizens should vote and have pointed out that they have an obilgation to do so.

3. The reason and excuses offered for not voting are not valid and are unworthy of a Christian.

application: We should inform ourselves as to the qualifications of candidates. We should know their views and what they stand for.

Background for Development:

introduction: Late in 1961, a papal audience was about to begin. The pilgrims were Germans, many of whom had saved for a long time to come to Rome. This was a dream fulfilled and an ambition realized. Suddenly, Pope John XIII appeared, with all the friendliness and charm he possessed. He began to speak to the enthusiastic audience. He began to speak in his informal and simple manner. Suddenly, he became more serious and grave in his talk. He reminded them that on that very day, elections were taking place in Germany. He reminded them of their duty to vote. Then he suggested that it might be better to participate in elections than to come on a pilgrimage to Rome. These words may strike us as surprising, but they remind us of something we don't always realize. We tend to overlook the fact that the right to vote also imposes an obligation to vote in a democratic society.

1. At first we might wonder why the Church should consider that voting is as important as all this. We might even wonder why the Church says anything at all about voting. The reason is that the Church, while remaining aloof from political differences among parties, sees clearly that matters affecting the Church, the family, education, the

poor, the aged, in short, all elements of society are affected by the actions of elected officials. Therefore, it is important that citizens in a society such as ours view their vote as a sacred duty, to be exercised when the opportunity arises to select our public officials. Citizens who vote intelligently are showing their concern for, their love of, all people because they are trying to establish good and honest government which will help people live in peace and harmony with justice for all.

2. Pope Pius XII offers another reason why individual responsibility in voting is important. One of the dangers of democratic society is the neglect of responsibility in civic life as well as the zeal to establish a just society. Since good government is not always self-perpetuating, a vigilant electorate is necessary in any modern society. Very often, the government which fails to serve the best interests of the citizens is the government which is selected by default.

The obligation of voting has been pointed out a lot by the popes. "The exercise of the right to vote is an act of serious moral responsibility, at least when it is a question of electing those who are called to give the country its constitution and laws...." (Pius XII, Allocution to the Sacred College, 16 March, 1946).

"It is a right and a duty to draw the attention of the faithful to the extraordinary importance of elections and the moral responsibility which rests on everyone who has a right to vote. Without any doubt, the Church intends to remain outside and above political parties, but how can she remain indifferent to the composition of a Parliament, when the Constitution gives it power to pass laws.... Then there are also other arduous questions, above all the problems and economic struggles which touch the well-being of the people. Insofar as they are of the temporal order (though in reality they also affect the moral order) Churchmen leave to others the care of pondering and treating technically with them for the common welfare of the nation. From all this it follows that:

"It is a strict duty for all who have the right to vote, men and women, to take apart in the elections. Everyone has to vote according to the dictates of his own conscience...." (Pope Pius XII, Address to the Delegates of the International Conference on Emigration, 17 October, 1951).

3. The percentage of people who exercise their right and duty of voting in the United States is far less than it is in many other countries. Some people fail to vote because of apathy. They simply do not take the trouble to go to the polls on election day. Others fail to vote because of cynicism. They regard politics as a dishonest busines and maintain that elections are "fixed." Still others fail to vote because they reason that their vote will make no difference among the millions of votes which will be cast.

None of these attitudes is worthy of a Christian. Since ours is a government of the people, each has a responsibility to see that the government is a good government. Each has an obligation of taking the trouble to go to the polls on election day. Cynicism is unworthy of a Christian, too. If there is dishonesty, it is not right merely to shrug one's shoulders. One should fight it. Dishonest politicians count on the cyncism of voters, which cynicism often is really an excuse for their own laziness. The person who reasons that his vote will not make any difference is wrong on two counts. First of all, it is the wrong philosophy. Each vote is important in itself as an exercise of one's political responsibility, sometimes as a protest. And secondly, the 1960 presidential election proved that this argument cannot be considered as valid. If one voter in a precinct in each state had changed his vote in that election, the result might well have been different than it was.

application: It is important not only to vote but to vote intelligently. To vote for a candidate without knowing what he stands for, without knowing what his qualifications are, is to vote irresponsibly. We should know what a candidate's convictions are. We should know how he will represent us on issues which affect the lives and welfare of people. The newspapers give us information about the voting records of congressmen. There are organizations which will gladly supply honest and objective information about candidates. We should take advantage of these services and make the effort which must be made if we are to vote intelligently and responsibly.

TWENTY - FOURTH SUNDAY AFTER PENTECOST

THE CORPORAL WORKS OF MERCY

aim: To show that the performance of the corporal works of mercy is still very possible in modern life and very necessary as a manifestation of Christian love.

suggested introduction: The story of the business man in Rome who collects food, clothing and money and brings them to the poor and homeless who live in the ancient ruins of Rome.

development: 1. Our Lord said that the criterion by which we will be judged is those expressions of Christian love which we call the corporal works of mercy.

2. These works of mercy are still very practicable today. We perform them by contributing to the charitable drives which are conducted every year and to the various collections. We must also perform them on the personal level.

application: There are people in need of help. We should make the effort to find them if we do not already know where they are.

Background for Development:

introduction: In the year following World War II, housing was extremely hard to find in many cities. Rome was no exception. People who worked and had money could find apartments or rooms. Those who could not work or who had no money could not find a place to sleep. Those who were old, homeless and friendless slept in doorways, in nooks and crannies which they found in the ancient ruins of Rome. A business man came upon one of those old people one night when he heard a groan coming from beneath his window. He found out that the old man had no place to go, no food, little clothing. He could not find the man a room, but he could and did bring him some food. Thus began a charitable work which is still going on today. Every night about midnight the man would take a bag of food and old clothing in his car and start his rounds. He would look for those poor, homeless people and give them what he could, a parcel of food, an old coat, a little money, a word of encouragement.

Here is a literal example of the performance of what we call the corporal works of mercy, those manifestations of love in practice according to which our Lord tells us He will judge us on the last day.

1. It is to be feared that we examine our conscience differently from the way the Lord will examine it for us when He judges us. We say, "Did I lie? Did I swear? Did I have bad thoughts?" The Lord will say, "Did you feed me when I was hungry? Did you clothe me? Did you see that I found shelter when I had no place to live? Did you visit me when I was in prison?" This is what our Lord Himself says that He will judge us on (cf. Matth. 25:34-40).

Our Lord speaks as if this is the only criterion by which we shall be judged. He says nothing about how many rosaries we might have said nor how many novenas we might have made, nothing even about the commandments of God and the Church. What this means is that saying prayers and keeping laws are not enough; we must love everyone; we must see Christ in everyone and actually treat every person as we would treat Christ Himself. We must practice the works of mercy.

2. These works of mercy are the essential expression of Christian love, yet they seem to many to be strangely unreal and impractical today.

How can you feed the hungry when everyone you know has enough to eat? How can you visit prisoners when they won't allow anyone but close relatives of the inmates inside the prison? How can you be expected to welcome into your home a stranger who might rob you or even kill you?

At the same time it is true that millions of people in the world are suffering from hunger and lack of clothing; millions of people are homeless or poorly housed. We do perform the works of mercy by contributing money and clothing to the various drives which are conducted every year. We do perform the works of mercy by contributing to the Charities collection. We even perform the works of mercy when we pay our taxes. The works of mercy apply to nations as well as to individuals. When our country gives aid to countries which have great problems of poverty, unemployment and overpopulation, whatever the motive of the officials, Christians should see that a work of mercy is being performed.

These contributions we make, however, even though right and necessary, are still impersonal. Should not the performance of the work of mercy involve a giving of oneself as well as the giving of money in a collection? Should there not be a personal involvement of some sort? How, in practice, does the modern Christian perform the works of mercy in a personal way?

It is to be remembered that when Christ said, "I was hungry and you gave me to eat" and "I was thirsty and you gave me to drink," He was speaking in the colorful, concrete oriental manner of speaking which was natural and familiar to Him and to His listeners. These works of mercy are examples rather than theological formulae. What Christ was really saying was, "I was in need and you came to my assistance." If it is a corporal work of mercy to give a drink to a thirsty man, why is it not also a corporal work of mercy to give a cigarette to someone who is "dying for a smoke?" If is is a corporal work of mercy to visit the sick, why is not also a corporal work of mercy to donate a used TV set to a lonely old lady? The catechism says that there are seven corporal works of mercy. It is hardly conceivable that Jesus was preoccupied with the number. Terminology is not what counts. Serving Christ in others and helping them, whatever their need, is what does count.

A Christian who is sensitive to the needs of others sees, without having to be told, that all about him are people who need his love and attention. There are couples who allow and encourage their teen-age daughters to act as baby-sitters only in cases where they will not be paid, giving a married couple a few hours of needed recreation. Many American couples are making it possible for young people of other countries to come here for an education by welcoming them into their homes as one of the family during the years of their schooling. There is even a way of visiting those in prison. Anyone who wishes to do so can aproach these groups existing in many areas who do a great work of finding employment for men who are to be released from prison.

application: There may be no people who are hungry or in need of clothing or a decent place to live in certain neighborhoods; there are many such people in other parts of our cities. There are plenty of families in need of direct and personal help in our poorer parishes. The priests in these parishes would be very happy to put anyone who is interested in contact with people who need help.

THANKSGIVING CLOTHING DRIVE

"I WAS NAKED AND YOU COVERED ME"

aim: To show that we can fulfill our obligation to help our brothers in need by contributing to the Bishops' Relief Clothing Drive.

suggested introduction: The story of the Maryknoll priest who visited a village but had nothing to give the people.

development: 1. God has blessed us here in America most abundantly. Two-thirds of the world is hungry and lacking in many of the essentials of life.

2. We must show our love for those who are in need. Our Lord makes this very clear. The pope reminds us.

application: In the Bishops' Relief Clothing Drive we are not asked to make a sacrifice of money, only to share what we have in our closets at home. Everyone—men, women and children—should contribute to this drive.

Background for Development:

introduction: Some years ago a Maryknoll priest was hitch-hicking on a dusty road in Bolivia. He was on his way to teach the children catechism in a nearby village. Luckily enough, the Bishops' Relief truck was on its way back after distributing clothes and food to the poor Indians. The driver was glad to drop the priest off in the village. As soon as the truck roared into the town-square, people came running from every house—it was the American Bishops' Relief truck.

Suddenly they fell silent. The truck rolled on. Politely, they listened and thanked him, but he saw that day the truth of those wise words of St. Thomas Aquinas—that a basic supply of the world's goods is necessary for a man to live a religious life. It does no good to preach to an empty stomach.

1. Very shortly, Thanksgiving Day will be here and it will be time to recall God's great blessings to us. We Americans rarely realize how wealthy we are compared to most of the other people on earth. We do not realize that many of our fellowmen don't have enough to eat, that children in many countries just south of our border have no clothes, no decent place to live. We have read this, we have seen it on television. We should realize it as we sit down to our delicious Thanksgiving dinner in our own warm homes, dressed in fine clothes. We should think of our fellow men, our fellow Christians, almost starving just a few hours away by jet plane.

2. Our Blessed Lord goes on to describe our last judgment and again He sets down one standard—"I was hungry and you gave me to eat, naked and you covered me—whatever you did to these the least of my brethren, you did it for me" (Matth. 25:35-40).

In his great letter "Mater et Magistra" (Christianity and Social Progress) our Holy Father Pope John makes the same point again and again. Foreign aid, properly administered by our nation, is simply human decency, basic Christianity. How can a nation continue to build larger barns to store its grain and stand by while millions starve? We have no choice as Ameriacns and Catholics but to support a legitimate foreign aid program by our government.

And yet Christian charity must be more than paying our taxes more or less willingly and so supporting foreign aid. It must be a personal sacrifice for the love of Christ in our fellow man. It means giving him something of our own freely, lovingly.

application: Very shortly we will begin our annual Bishops' Relief Clothing Drive. Each member of every family has his or her own wardrobe. There are shoes by the thousands in every parish that are still good but will rarely be worn again. There are warm clothes in good repair which are gathering dust in closets in every home. Each person from the smallest child to grandma, has his or her part to play in this collection. In his book "Parent and Child" Father Leo Trese mentions what an important lesson this clothing drive can be for a small child in learning thoughtfulness and love of others. For a change, no one is asked to give a cent in this collection. They are simply asked to share with others some of the things with which God has blessed them—the usable clothing they can easily sacrifice for God's poor.

We all know the story of St. Martin of Tours. St Martin was a young French soldier riding along on his fine horse with his beautiful military cape flowing in the wind behind. Suddenly, at a bend in the road, he saw a poor man crouched in rags freezing in the cold. Martin stopped, drew his sword and slashed his fine cape in two. He wrapped the poor man in half, keeping the other half for himself. That very night the exhausted soldier saw a beautiful vision in his tent—Christ Our Lord stood silently smiling on Martin, wrapped in the half cape he had given the beggar.,

"I was naked and you covered me. Whatever you did for the least of these my brethren, you did for me" (Matth. 25:40).

Give Instructions as to Time and Place of Collection.

PETER'S PENCE

OUR HOLY FATHER

aim: To recall the importance of the papacy as the seat of unity and teaching authority within the Church, and to urge the people to show their loyalty to the Holy Father in the Peter's Pence collection.

suggested introduction: The more than three million pilgrims who visited Rome during the Holy Year of 1950 caught a glimpse of the marvelous unity within the Church, centered in the Pope.

development: 1. The Pope, as Vicar of Christ, is the person in whom unity is centered in the Church.

2. The Pope is the great teacher, applying the teachings of Christ to issues and problems of the day.

application: We should express our loyalty to the Holy Father by praying for him and by contributing to the Peter's Pence collection.

Background for Development:

introduction: More than three million pilgrims of all nationalities and races made their way to Rome during the Holy Year of 1950. Most of these people, especially those who came from distant places, gained a deeper appreciation of something which they had known before but never fully realized, the wonderful unifying force that is the papacy. In a world torn apart by opposing forces, they saw what the unity of Catholicism means, the brotherly harmony which has existed for twenty centuries. They saw the person who is the center of that unity and harmony, the vicar of Jesus Christ, our Holy Father, the Pope.

1. The First Vatican Council expressed the role of the Holy Father as the principle of unity within the Church: "The eternal shepherd and bishop of our souls, in order to confer a perennial character on the saving work of redemption, ordained the building of the Holy Church, in which, as in the abode of the living God, all the faithful should be included by the bond of one faith and charity. To this end, before He was glorified, He prayed to His Father, not only for the Apostles but also for those who by their word were to believe in Him, that they should be one, as the Son himself and the Father are one. Just as He sent out the Apostles whom He had chosen from the world, and as He himself had been sent by the Father, so He wished to have shepherds and teachers in His Church even unto the consummation of the world. But in order that the episcopacy should be one and indivisible, and so that, by mutual agreement amongst the priests, the whole multitude of believers should be kept in the unity of faith and communion, He established blessed Peter above the other Apostles and thus, instituted in him, the principle and the visible and the perpetual foundation of both these unities, on the solidity of which the eternal temple will be raised, and the sublimity of the Church destined for heaven will be made safe in the firmness of this faith."

The Second Vatican Council, "following closely in the footsteps of the First Vatican Council," complemented the teaching of that Council and decreed that "Jesus Christ, the eternal Shepherd, established His Holy Church, having sent forth the Apostles as He himself had been sent by the Father (John 20:21); He willed that their successors, namely the Bishops, should be shepherds in His Church even to the consummation of the world. And in order that the episcopate itself might be one and undivided, He placed Blessed Peter over the other Apostles and instituted in him a permanent and visible source and foundation of unity of faith and communion." The Council went on to propound the principle of collegiality or the teaching that just as in the Gospel St. Peter and the other Apostles constituted one Apostolic college, so in a similar way the Roman Pontiff, the successor of Peter, and the Bishops, the successors of the Apostles, are joined together. "But the college or body of Bishops has no authority unless it is understood together with the Roman Pontiff, the successor of Peter, as its head. The Pope's power of primacy over all, both pastors and faithful, remains whole and intact. In virtue of his office, that is as Vicar of Christ and pastor of the whole Church, the Roman Pontiff has full, supreme and universal power over the Church. And he is always free to exercise this power."

Jesus told the Apostles that He would not leave them orphans. He said these words, referring to the Holy Spirit whom He would send to dwell within them. But in another sense, too, Christ has not left us orphans. He Himself has remained among us. He has remained in the Eucharist, the sacramental bond of love and unity in His Mystical Body. He has remained in His vicar, the Holy Father, the person in whom the unity and harmony and love within the Church are centered.

2. The Pope is the great teacher. As vicar of Christ he applies the eternal truths which Jesus Christ teaches to the conditionsof the times. All throughout the history of the Church the Popes have fulfilled this essential teaching office. In more recent times, with the ever increasing complexity of life, they have been more and more articulate, pointing out how men are to love one another by the practice of justice and charity. Pope Leo XIII was a great revolutionary in his day—a time when the industrial revolution had brought about great changes and also given rise to serious social evils. This great Pope fearlessly taught the Christian doctrine on social justice at a time when there was great opposition to it. Pope Pius X brought the people in the Church into closer contact with Christ in the Eucharist. Pius XI, like Leo XIII, was a great teacher on social matters. He recalled the teachings of Leo and brought them abreast of his time. Pius XII was a great teacher in an incredible number of fields. He was fully aware of the manifold problems of modern life and tireless in applying to them the teachings of Christ. In a world torn by war he was above all the Pope of Peace, who called upon all men to live in peace as brothers and children of God. Pope John XXIII has clearly shown his Christ-like longing for unity among men, especially among the followers of Christ. He has constantly striven to promote the re-union of all Christians within the Body of Christ. His love for all—for people of all faiths—has been so evident that men of all faiths have come to take a new view of the papacy. John XXIII, too, has not shrunk from the task of applying the teachings of Christ to modern social conditions. His great encyclical, Christianity and Social Progress, treated of the questions of the ownership and distribution of property, its social function and the social responsibility which is rooted in the right of private property. It treated of the new aspects of the social question, urbanization, diminishment of agriculture, automation, population increase and economic development, emerging nations, inequalities between the nations of the world. Teaching the love of Christ, Pope John reminded all Christians that not only individuals but nations as well must practice charity, that nations which are highly industrialized must give the benefit of their experience

and skill in helping under-developed nations to industrialize and must help the poor, the needy, the under-privileged all over the world.

application: We look to the Holy Father for leadership and guidance. He is Christ among us. We profess our personal loyalty to him. We pray for the Pope in every Mass. He is constantly calling for our prayers. We should pray for him and for his many intentions frequently indeed. The Peter's Pence collection provides a way of expressing our loyalty to the Holy Father. Here is something which is not a tax but a free-will offering. Few people realize the great number of appeals which are made to the Pope for charity. One of the great uses to which the Pope puts the money he receives in the Peter's Pence collection is works of charity. In giving to the Peter's Pence collection, therefore, we are showing our loyalty to the Holy Father and also contributing to our needy brothers and sisters in Christ.

SEMINARIANS' SUPPORT

THE SEMINARY COLLECTION

aim: To encourage the people to contribute generously toward the support of seminarians or (if the Diocese has got a seminary) to the seminary collection as a sign of their love for the priesthood.

suggested introduction: At the Last Supper, our Lord showed His love by giving us not only the Eucharist but also the sacred priesthood, by which He continues His work in the world.

development: 1. The priest is a man who has dedicated himself and his whole life to the loving service of others.

2. American Catholics show their love for the priesthood by encouraging their sons to be priests and by supporting seminaries.

application: Contribute to the seminary collection (next Sunday).

Background for Development:

introduction: St. John begins his account of the Last Supper with the words: "Before the feast of the Passover, Jesus knowing that his hour had come, to pass out of this world to the Father, having loved his own who were in the world, loved them to the end." The great manifestation of Christ's love was the Eucharist, by which He gave Himself as He would give Himself on the cross. But closely connected with the Eucharist and always associated with it, is another precious gift of Christ, the sacred priesthood. Through the priesthood, Christ shares with men the awesome powers which are His as the great High Priest. Through the priesthood, Christ gives to His Church, "other Christs," who continue His work on earth.

1. The priesthood is one of the great manifestations of Christ's love for His Church. It is also the means whereby men in the Church express their love for the children of God, the members of the Church.

Catholics are inclined to take the love of the priest for granted, just as people in general are apt to take the love of parents for granted. They expect the priest to be at their service at all times, for consultation in time of sorrow or trouble, to give them the sacraments, at any hour of the day or night in cases of emergency. They expect him to be kind and patient, not only in the confessional, but at all times. They expect him to be self-sacrificial, to be available, approachable and always generous with his time. It is well that this is so. The fact that Catholics accept the love of the priest as a matter of course and simply expect it to be there speaks well for the priesthood itself and is a tribute to priests. It shows that people realize what a priest is—a man who has dedicated himself and his whole life to loving service of his brothers and sisters of Christ within the Body of Christ.

People outside the Church sometimes think that the religious lives of Catholics are complicated unnecessarily by the fact of their having to deal so much with priests. "How simple just to confess your sins to God," "How much more direct to speak to God yourself instead of having a priest pray for you." But Catholics know well the great consolation and help which the priest brings them. They can and do confess their sins directly to God. They can and do pray all by themselves. But they also know the assurance and comfort which can only come from the advice and absolution of a priest in the confessional. They know the great consolation of having a priest at the bedside of their loved ones, saying the age old prayers of the Church for the sick and the dying and bringing Christ Himself into their homes. They know, with great relief, that there is always someone to whom they can go with their troubles, someone who will listen to them when no one else is willing to. It would be a rare Catholic who could not look back and recall times in his life when a priest, with the love of Jesus Christ, helped him in a time of special trouble or suffering.

2. American Catholics show the high regard they have for the priesthood by encouraging their sons to become priests. In some countries parents do their best to prevent their sons from entering the priesthood, but here a family is proud to have a son a priest. Every American diocese has its share of young men studying to be priests. Although some have large numbers of seminarians, there are hardly any which can supply enough priests for their needs. The demand for priests in America and elsewhere in the world is growing faster than the supply of vocations coming from the seminaries. The people of the United States show their love for the priesthood by digging down into their pockets to provide the money which gives our seminarians the best possible education for the priesthood.

        application: If priests show their love for God's people, as they do in their ministry, the people, in turn, should show their love for their priests by supporting the seminaries, without which there would be no priests.

ALBA HOUSE is staffed by the Pauline Fathers and Brothers. All the operations going into the making of this book were carried out by the Fathers and Brothers as part of their publishing apostolate. The Society of St. Paul was founded to work exclusively in communications. By this is meant that it was instituted to spread the teachings of Christ via the press, radio, motion pictures and television.

PAULINES reach thousands daily — by each book, pamphlet, production — multiplying the good message and carrying it into all manner of places. It is their job in the Church to staff editorial offices, publishing plants, film studios, etc., and to develop those fields of communications still comparatively un-touched for Christ.

PAULINES, aside from living a balanced religious life, perform their apostolic work according to their talents and training as: editors, designers, directors, proofreaders, writers, artists, photographers, pressmen, typesetters, binders; compositors, photoengravers, as well as in many other editorial and technical fields. The **Vatican Council's** decree on the media of social communications has been a great source of renewed energy for them.

INTERNATIONAL as the air-waves, the Pauline Fathers and Brothers are located in twenty-three countries, with headquarters in Rome. In the United States they are in New York City, Boston, Buffalo, Detroit, and Youngstown.

A BROCHURE on the Society and its aims can be obtained for yourself, or any young man whom you feel might qualify to become a Pauline Priest or Brother, by simply sending a card to: The Pauline Fathers and Brothers, Vocation Office, 2187 Victory Blvd., Staten Island, N. Y. (212-GI 2-0047)